THE 1896 LIGHT RAILWAYS ACT

THE 1896 LIGHT RAILWAYS ACT

THE LAW THAT MADE HERITAGE RAILWAYS POSSIBLE

John Hannavy

AMBERLEY

Title page: A wooden-bodied ex-NER/LNER carriage under restoration at Steamtown, Carnforth, Lancashire, in the late 1970s. Steamtown had a short demonstration track and was authorised to run passenger shuttle services under the Steamtown Light Railway Order of 1973. The site is now operated as the main depot for West Coast Railways.

Opposite: Two of the several souvenir postcards published by the Campbeltown & Machrihanish Light Railway in 1908, the year the 2-foot 3-inch-gauge line started operating passenger services.

First published 2019

Amberley Publishing
The Hill, Stroud
Gloucestershire, GL5 4EP

www.amberley-books.com

Copyright © John Hannavy, 2019

The right of John Hannavy to be identified as the Author of this work has been asserted in accordance with the Copyrights, Designs and Patents Act 1988.

ISBN 978 1 4456 9344 6 (print)
ISBN 978 1 4456 9345 3 (ebook)

British Library Cataloguing in Publication Data.
A catalogue record for this book is available from the British Library.

Typesetting by Aura Technology and Software Services, India. Printed in the UK.

Contents

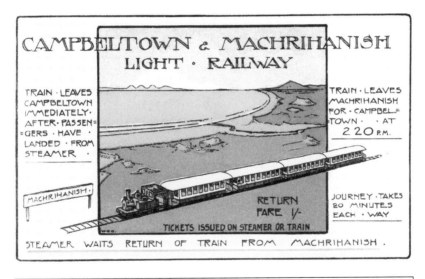

LOADING LUGGAGE AT THE MACHRIHANISH TERMINUS.

A Southern Railways U Class 2-6-0 Mogul approaching Norden station on the Swanage Railway, August 2018. Built in Brighton in 1926 as a 2-6-4 'River' or K Class tank engine for the Southern, the locomotive was rebuilt two years later as a 2-6-0 Mogul. Withdrawn by BR in 1964, it spent twelve years in Woodham Brothers scrapyard in Barry before being rescued and restored at the Mid-Hants Railway. It is now steamed regularly on the Swanage Railway.

Introduction

In no other country in the world is there anything to match Britain's love affair with the steam train; nowhere else are there so many preserved railways keeping the magic of steam alive – and the number is still growing. That seems entirely appropriate – after all, Britain was the birthplace both of the railway itself, and of the noble art of trainspotting.

For the past fifty years and more, enthusiasts have retrieved the rusting hulks of long-abandoned steam locomotives from scrapyards across the country and lovingly coaxed them back to life. The most famous scrapyard of them all – Woodham Brothers in Barry – has now been stripped of every locomotive it ever held, and just about every serviceable spare part. In total, 213 locomotives were salvaged from that one yard alone – the last only leaving in 1990 – with more than half of them currently back in steam and running on heritage lines across the country today.

So famous has Woodham's scrapyard become that several books have been written about it, and a museum telling its story, and the crucial part it played in the history of the railway preservation, is being considered.

Great Western Railway 6000 Class No. 6023 *King Edward II* – built at Swindon Works in 1930 – looking very sorry for itself in Woodham Brothers scrapyard in Barry in the late 1970s, having been there since 1962. It would not be rescued until 1985, the 150th anniversary of the GWR, when Harvey's of Bristol towed it to Temple Meads station. It was eventually moved to Didcot to start a twenty-year complete rebuild, moving under its own power in 2011 for the first time in nearly half a century. Note in this photograph that the rear driving wheels have been cut.

LMS Jubilee 4-6-0 *Galatea*, bearing British Railways number 45699, languished in Barry scrapyard for fifteen years before being rescued, by which time the locomotive had been stripped of just about anything that would prove useful on other restoration projects. Built at Crewe in 1936 and classified by the LMS as 5XP – later classed by BR as 6P – it was withdrawn from service at the end of 1964 and moved to Barry in 1965, remaining at Woodham Brothers until 1980. *Galatea* was eventually rebuilt and returned to main line steam in 2013 by West Coast Railways. The yellow diagonal stripe on the cab – only added in late 1964 – signified that the locomotive was prohibited from working under the 25 kV overhead wires on the newly electrified sections of the West Coast Main Line south of Crewe.

Some preserved locomotives have already spent more than five times as many years running on heritage lines than they ever spent in regular British Railways service. A notable example, BR Class 9F No. 92203 *Black Prince*, built at Swindon in 1959 and withdrawn in 1967 after only eight and half years in service, has spent the last forty-five years hauling passenger trains on a number of heritage lines. Now based on the North Norfolk Railway, it will hopefully continue to do so for many years to come.

All this has come about largely because of a piece of almost-forgotten legislation – our heritage railways collectively benefitting from a very welcome, but entirely unintended, consequence of an Act of Parliament passed more than a century ago.

The 'law of unintended consequences' as an idea can be traced back centuries and has been applied to all sorts of legislation, intended for one purpose, which turns out to have an effect the legislators could never have anticipated. Sometimes the effect of such a law has been detrimental, other times – perhaps more rarely – highly beneficial.

Adam Smith (1727–90), the Scottish philosopher and economist who wrote *The Wealth of Nations*, was just one of those who counselled that lawmakers should not seek to enact their legislation until every possible outcome of it had been carefully thought through. Similar views had been expressed by the English philosopher John Locke nearly a century earlier, but neither man could have foreseen the recurrent 'unintended consequences' of the laws that would be passed in the centuries which followed them.

Above: Railway enthusiasts talk to the driver as Swindon-built ex-GWR *Hinton Manor* prepares to leave Hampton Load station on the Severn Valley Railway in the mid-1990s.

Below: 9F No. 92203 *Black Prince* at Holt on the North Norfolk Railway in 2015, with a mid-morning train from Sheringham. Withdrawn from BR service in Birkenhead in November 1967, just ten months after being given a full heavy overhaul, No. 92203 was bought directly from British Railways by the artist David Shepherd.

A notable example in recent decades was intended to conserve fish stocks by limiting the catches fishermen were allowed to land. The unintended consequence, however, resulted in thousands of tons of dead fish being thrown back into the sea for fear of breaching quotas and incurring crippling fines. Nobody had considered that.

British Railways Ivatt Class 2, 2-6-0 No. 46512, built at Swindon in 1952, pulls the first train of the day from Aviemore into Boat of Garten station on the Strathspey Railway in 2017. Next stop is Broomhill.

Nobody could have foreseen the unintended impact of the Light Railways Act of 1896, but rather than having an unhappy consequence, it has proved far more beneficial than those who promoted it could ever have imagined – especially as it was only intended as a temporary measure to help complete the Victorian railway network by bringing low-cost railways to communities in out-of-the-way rural locations.

Luckily for us, it was never repealed. The fact that we can board a steam train at any one of the dozens of heritage lines which are dotted across the country – more than half a century after Dr Richard Beeching believed he had sounded the death knell of steam traction in his 1963 report *The Reshaping of British Railways* – is an unintended but very welcome consequence of that 1896 Act. This book explores its fascinating story.

John Hannavy, 2019

The author on the regulator of Hudswell Clarke 0-6-0ST No. 813 – built for Port Talbot Docks in 1901 – during the locomotive's visit to the East Somerset Railway in 2008.

Thomas the Tank Engine Day on the Bo'ness & Kinneil Railway in Scotland in 2009 draws huge crowds, introducing live steam to new generations. Here, the sole survivor of the LNER, D49 Class 4-4-0 No. 246 *Morayshire* – double-heading a train with Riddles BR Standard Class 4 tank No. 80105 – wears a Thomas face for the occasion.

Building the Victorian Railway Network

B ritain's railway infrastructure was largely complete long before the end of the nineteenth century, and creating the network had employed hundreds of thousands of men, often working under the most appalling of conditions.

The engineering challenges which the railways posed were enormous, often driving engineers to develop new and innovative solutions to the challenges they faced in cutting their iron and steel swathes through the British landscape.

Construction challenges, however, represented only some of the hurdles that Victorian railway builders had to surmount. Before work on every new railway even started, its backers had to seek parliamentary approval – every new line required a separate Act of Parliament – and rights of way had to be negotiated with landowners, several of whom were vehemently opposed to the railways crossing their properties.

The most prolific period of railway building had been the 1840s and 1850s, when the major trunk routes were laid. But with no overall railway strategy ever being worked out for the country as a whole, it developed into a competitive free-for-all, with multiple routes being built for getting from A to B in several cases – each at huge expense.

Every large city finished up with several railway stations, and sometimes rival companies opened two or more even in relatively small towns. In some places they were built virtually next door to each other.

Above: The Glen Ogle Viaduct was built by the Callander & Oban Railway, opening in 1870. The line closed in 1965 and the twelve-arch viaduct is now part of the Rob Roy Footpath.

Opposite: Isambard Kingdom Brunel's Royal Albert Bridge across the Tamar at Saltash, opened in 1859, is an engineering marvel. His innovative 'Lenticular Truss' design provided all the strength of a suspension bridge without the need for cable anchors.

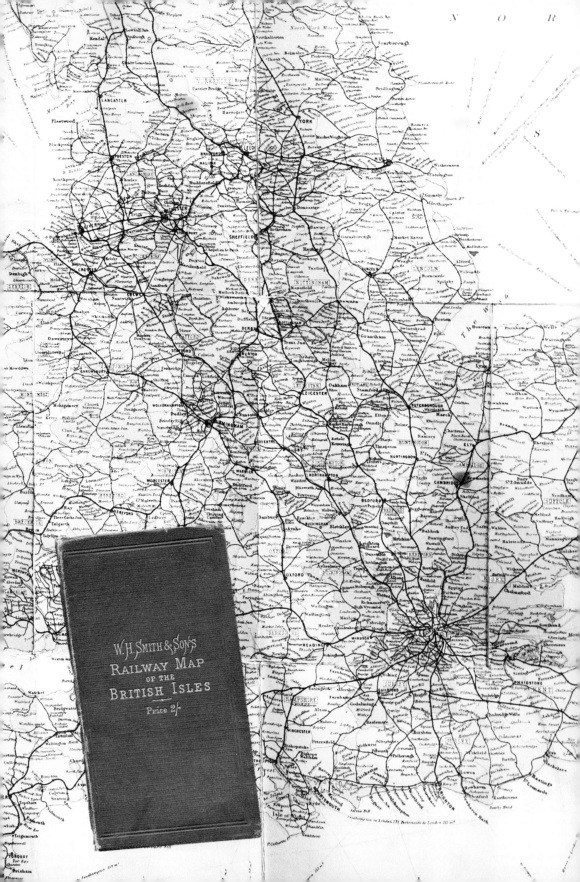

Each company sought access to the major centres, resulting in the duplication of services. In Manchester, for example, there were four main line stations operated by four separate companies, with three of them – each with their own large and impressive station buildings – all competing for passengers to the same destination: London.

It would not be until the 1960s that all London traffic would be handled from a single terminus: Manchester Piccadilly. That, of course, brought with it the loss of one of the most scenic routes south, from Manchester Central through the Peak District.

Of the many hundreds of railway companies that were established with such high hopes, a number survived only a few years before hitting the financial buffers and being taken over by larger operators. Indeed some failed before even the first sod had been cut, the whole process of seeking official approval having used up most of their working capital. There were even a few which disappeared without trace, without ever leaving a mark on the landscape.

While many other railway lines built in Victorian times have long since been abandoned – either as a result of Beeching's axe or simply because they were based on flawed and overambitious business plans and doomed to failure from the outset – they have all left their marks across Britain as footpaths, cycle paths, or just overgrown bridges and embankments.

Above: A Raphael Tuck postcard, published for the London & North Western Railway and used in 1905 showing Crewe Junction looking north. The complex signalling and track work in and out of Crewe station was radically modified in the 1980s and 1990s – that work was required to replace outdated signalling, some of which dated back to the late nineteenth century. At the same time the number of diamond crossings was reduced from fifty-six to four, and the number of point ends from 229 to 106. Now, with the advent of HS2, further extensive reconstruction of the tracks into the station will be needed, with one proposal even suggesting moving the station 2 miles out of Crewe itself. A more likely outcome will be a radical rebuild of the nineteenth-century station itself, perhaps with additional platforms.

Opposite: When W. H. Smith & Son published this railway map towards the end of the nineteenth century, the railway network was almost complete. Comparing it with today's railway route map really does give a sense of the enormous scale of railway construction across the country in Victorian times – and how much has subsequently been lost.

Central Station, Manchester.

Above and left: By the end of the nineteenth century, services to London from Manchester were available from three competing railway companies and their three stations. The Great Central Railway ran services out of Manchester London Road (known as Manchester Piccadilly since 1960). The London & North Western Railway operated trains from their Manchester Exchange station serving routes to London Euston, Liverpool, Wigan, Bolton, Huddersfield, Leeds, Hull and Newcastle among others. After Exchange's closure in 1969, all Euston services were rerouted to start and terminate at Piccadilly. From 1890, the Midland Railway ran its London services out of Manchester Central, operated by the Cheshire Lines Committee – seen here in a 1908 postcard (above) and as a derelict ruin in the early 1970s (right). It was later used as a car park for several years before being restored as an exhibition and conference centre. Known as G-Mex for a number of years, the centre has now reverted to its historic name, Manchester Central. The station's architect was none other than Sir John Fowler of Forth Bridge fame.

Developing locomotives and rolling stock was one thing, but designing and building the cuttings, tunnels and bridges through, and on which, the trains would run was of a different order. That many of the lines, bridges and tunnels constructed more than a century and a half ago are still in use today is a testament to the skills of their engineers.

It can be reasonably argued that the proliferation of bridges in the nineteenth century had an even more enduring impact on the British landscape than the railway lines themselves. Their imposing presence was impossible to ignore, so it says a great deal about their design and construction that so many of them are now seen as enhancing the landscape rather than detracting from it. But their cost was sometimes a major factor in determining whether or not a particular route could be constructed economically.

The range of bridge styles was considerable – from simple single spans across roadways, to massive multi-arch viaducts spanning wide valleys. But these new intrusions into the landscape were not universally appreciated.

The art historian and critic John Ruskin hated the Forth Bridge, suggesting it would have been better had he been born blind than have to look at it, and William Morris described it as the 'extremest specimen of all ugliness'. A century and a quarter later, we cannot imagine the Firth of Forth without it.

Many of the permanent railway bridges which were constructed across the country seemed to push engineering ingenuity to new heights – quite literally.

The Crumlin Viaduct is a notable example. Designed by Thomas Kennard and opened in 1857, it was built to carry the Taff Vale Extension of the Newport,

Dwarfed by the sheer scale of the structure, a ScotRail multiple unit crosses the Forth Bridge in 2016, almost unseen. While the bridge is still an essential part of the East Coast Main Line, it is quite lightly used – except at peak times when there are around five trains an hour in each direction.

Manchester Exchange station, built by the London & North Western Railway and opened in 1884, hosted their London services. Previously the company's London trains had departed from Manchester Victoria.

Abergavenny & Hereford Railway across the valleys of the Ebbw and Kendon rivers in South Wales. The sheer audacity of the bridge was breathtaking, its design innovative and its scale impressive, and at 61 metres (200 feet) high and with a span of 500 metres (1,650 feet), it posed enormous engineering challenges, while solving others.

Crumlin Viaduct from Canal.

Above: The Crumlin Viaduct's long life vindicated its builders' faith in the cast-iron Warren Truss design, standing strong against the elements until dismantled in 1965.

Below: The 'Cornish Riviera Express' awaits departure from Penzance station *c*. 1910, while beyond it stands a Swindon-built GWR 3252 Duke Class locomotive designed by William Dean. A large number of these 4-4-0 locomotives were built between 1895 and 1899.

A stone bridge was considered both too expensive and unsuitable for the high winds which swept down the valleys, so the decision was made to construct it out of cast iron, thus substantially reducing both the structure's wind resistance and its construction and maintenance costs. The result was the highest viaduct ever constructed in Britain, and the third highest anywhere in the world.

The cast ironwork came from the Falkirk Iron Company, with wrought iron supplied by the Blaenavon Iron & Coal Company. Both companies were owned by Kennard. A third company, Crumlin Viaduct Works, was responsible for the on-site assembly. The Crumlin Viaduct Works Company went on to enjoy considerable success, manufacturing the ironwork for Joseph Cubitt's Blackfriars Bridge in London, and also diversified into the design and manufacture of railway signalling and switchgear.

The whole structure was completed for an estimated £62,000 and to load test the bridge, six locomotives laden with pig iron or lead – with a total weight of 380 tons – were run on to one of the spans, and then repeatedly moved across and back while careful measurements were made of the changes in the girder's deflection.

The volunteer driver from Pontypool who carried out the load test became known as 'Mad Jack' – perhaps not surprisingly as he had been the only volunteer to come forward for this risky exercise.

While cost was clearly a consideration in the construction of the Crumlin Viaduct, it was a significant factor in Isambard Kingdom Brunel's designs for the many viaducts that were required in the building of the Cornwall Railway west from Plymouth. The quasi-independent Cornwall Railway was backed by the Great Western, the Bristol & Exeter Railway and the South Devon Railway, each of whom contributed to the construction costs.

Testing a bridge on the London & North Western Railway, from the company's 'Revised Series' of Edwardian postcards published in November 1904. The location of the bridge cannot be identified, but it has been suggested that it might be in the Bolton area. The load to which it was being subjected – six 0-6-2T Coal Tanks designed by Francis Webb and built at Crewe between 1881 and 1887 – constituted a combined weight of around 270 tons.

Although authorised by parliament in 1846, work did not start on the broad gauge line for several years, eventually opening to Truro in 1859 and to Falmouth by 1863. At the outset Brunel had advised that the savings in construction costs would bring increased maintenance costs as the pine fans and bridge decks would require specialist annual treatment to avoid deterioration.

Left: The original Olive Mount Cutting on the Liverpool & Manchester Railway had two tracks and opened in 1830. Designed by George Stephenson, it was widened in 1871 to take four tracks into Liverpool's Lime Street station. It was cut with little more than pickaxes, shovels and the odd stick of dynamite. This is one of a series of London & North Western Railway postcards published in January 1905.

Below: London's Euston station was the southern terminus of the London & North Western Railway. In Charles Hooper & Company's *ABC Guide to London* – which had by then sold 700,000 copies – it is listed under 'E' as 'Euston Station, Terminus of the London & North Western Railway', while in the same volume, under 'L' for 'London & North Western Railway', it is still listed as 'Euston Square', which had been its original name.

The woodwork was assembled at a specially built facility at Lostwithiel, where the timber arrived by boat and was cut to size and treated. The wood was preserved with the application of either mercuric chloride (Kyanising) or zinc chloride (Burnettising), named after their inventors in the 1830s, John Howard Kyan and William Burnett respectively. The two longest of these hybrid viaducts were both built in Truro – the twenty-pier Carvedras Viaduct and the fifteen-pier Truro or Moresk Viaduct. Both were replaced in the early years of the last century – Carvedras in 1902 and Truro in 1904. The piers of Brunel's originals still stand alongside several of the replacement brick arch viaducts. The replacement of some of them coincided with the planned doubling of parts of the single-track broad gauge line with the twin-tracked standard gauge track which still operates today. Brunel's bridges would have been neither wide enough nor strong enough to support the increased operational stresses of those planned developments.

Despite concerns about their durability, a few of these highly original viaducts survived into the 1930s, the last to go being the eleven-arch Carnon Viaduct in August 1933 and the fourteen-arch Collegewood Viaduct in July the following year.

Given that building these monumental structures often stretched engineering know-how to new limits in an era when a disregard of health and safety was the norm, it is not surprising that there was a significant loss of life, and many serious injuries to the workforce. However, with a few very notable exceptions, the bridges themselves, once completed, proved hugely reliable.

Brunel's unusual design for his viaducts on the Cornwall Railway was evolved to reduce costs. The route required the crossing of a large number of rivers and valleys, and forty-two viaducts were built to this unusual hybrid design of stone piers and supporting wooden fans. They proved expensive to maintain and by 1933 all were replaced by more conventional stone arched spans. The fifteen piers of Truro's Carvedras Viaduct still stand alongside the new 1902 bridge.

The two extremes of scale for stations – an Edwardian postcard of London's Liverpool Street station *c.* 1910 (top), with a James Holden/ Frederick Russell-designed Great Eastern Railway S46 Class 4-4-0 in steam and the short single platform at St Winefride's Halt on the 1.75-mile branch line between Holywell Town and Holywell Junction in Wales (middle). Opened in 1863 by the Holywell Railway, it ran as a push-pull service with an 0-6-2T locomotive and two coaches. The station was closed in 1954.

Carnforth station on the busy West Coast Main line was built by the Lancaster & Carlisle Railway, but by the time this view was published, it was operated by the London & North Western Railway, which had absorbed the L&CR. It was later used as the setting for David Lean's classic film *Brief Encounter* starring Celia Johnson and Trevor Howard and based on Noel Coward's play *Still Lives*. The nearby Carnforth Motive Power Depot – Shed 10A – was home to the famous 'Steamtown' museum from 1969 until the late 1990s.

The failure of Thomas Bouch's Tay Bridge in 1879 is the most infamous, its infamy stretching well into the twentieth-century postcard era, with Valentines of Dundee turning their archive of photographs of the disaster into an extensive catalogue of postcards aimed squarely at collectors. Some of those cards were clearly intended to underline (rather unfairly) the frailty of Bouch's original bridge.

One of the most bizarre stories, however, relates to the building of the Loch nan Uamh Viaduct by 'Concrete Bob' McAlpine on Scotland's West Highland line, which was opened in 1901. The concrete piers of the eight-arch bridge were in the process of being filled with rubble when a horse and cart carrying some of the rubble fell into the void in the central pier. Recent scanning of the bridge found the remains of the horse and cart still embedded deep inside.

Where in the past the only need for a bridge had been where a road crossed a river or a canal, the railways required the construction of thousands of bridges and viaducts – over roads, canals and rivers, across gorges, under roads and over other railway lines. The range and complexity of the geological and topographical challenges which railway builders had to deal with pushed engineering to new limits, including coming to terms with new materials and – with metal bridges – the seasonal changing geometry of, and stresses on, the bridges themselves.

McAlpine's most famous bridge is the 30-metre-high Glenfinnan Viaduct, the largest concrete arch bridge in the world at the time of its opening in 1901. It has twenty-one arches in its 380-metre length, taking the West Highland line around a graceful curve over the River Finnan. It, too, remains a popular subject for today's photographers.

The new art of photography was, by the 1850s, regularly called upon to chronicle the construction of many of the routes. Some of the larger companies – such as the London & North Western Railway – later used their archives of early photography chronicling their heritage to create historical sets of postcards for Edwardian collectors.

Southern Railway 4-6-0 No. 850 *Lord Nelson* – designed by Richard Maunsell and built in 1926 as the first of a class of sixteen locomotives – standing in front of the coaling towers outside Shed 10A, Carnforth, in the 1980s. Part of the National Collection, *Lord Nelson* is currently undergoing a major rebuild at Ropley on the Mid-Hants Railway.

The Caledonian Railway's Doune station was rebuilt in 1905. While the village of Doune, with its medieval castle, was on the busy tourist line between Dunblane, Callander and the Trossachs, a station on this scale was a bold statement. It was closed in 1965 and demolished in 1968.

Ystradowen station, opened by the Cowbridge Railway in 1865 with one platform and a passing loop beyond it, was the sort of lightly used route which the 1896 Light Railways Act was later designed to encourage. From *c.*1904 the line was served by steam railcars or by auto-train – a tank engine coupled to a single driving coach for push-pull operation.

Colwall station in Herefordshire today bears little resemblance to the station seen in this 1907 postcard. Now just a single platform offers services to Paddington and Birmingham.

The scale and success of the achievements of the original railway builders, designers, surveyors, architects and workforce, can be recognised as monumental when compared with the challenges, cost over-runs and delays which seem to accompany every modernisation programme on the network more than a century and a half later.

Today's railways suffer from a number of unique factors, not least of which being their age, and because of under-investment over the years that infrastructure has changed very little since the mid-nineteenth century.

That antiquity brings with it enormous challenges when belated modernisation schemes are being undertaken, and today's emphasis on the health and safety of the workforce while upgrading a working railway imposes additional responsibilities.

Whereas the original railway builders were cutting through virgin landscapes with few regulations to hamper their progress, today's workforce updating the railway has

Exiting Haverthwaite tunnel on the former Furness Railway branch line to Lakeside in the early 1980s, Hunslet 0-6-0T *Cumbria* puts on a fine display for the camera. The line was opened in 1869, closed to passenger traffic in 1965 and to freight in 1967, and was reopened as a heritage railway in 1973.

to operate safely – either around a busy train timetable, or during night-time closures of sections of the line, slowing progress markedly.

During the upgrade, Network Rail suggested that the (now only partial) electrification of the Great Western line was years late and several times over budget because of the complexity of making way for the overhead cabling in Isambard Kingdom Brunel's Box Tunnel in Wiltshire. The work involved lowering the trackbed by several feet to

The Category A listed nineteen-span Leaderfoot Viaduct was opened in 1863 and carried the Berwickshire Railway across the River Tweed in the Scottish Borders, thus creating a link between the North British Railway's east coast line to York and their Waverley Route from Edinburgh to Carlisle. The line was closed to passengers in 1948 and to freight in 1965.

Blackburn station, Lancashire. The two glass-roofed train sheds, one of which is seen here, had to be removed due to their parlous state of repair during a modernisation of the station in 2000.

Early on 19 December 1906, a goods train approaching Blairgowrie station from Coupar Angus was derailed at points just outside the town where the local branch line to Blairgowrie left the main line. The forty-wagon train was hauled by Caledonian Railway's Drummond 0-6-0 No. 590 *Jumbo Goods*, running tender first. While wreckage littered the tracks, the train's cargo of whisky was undamaged!

make space for the overhead catenary. The upgrade took almost as long as the original planned timescale for cutting the tunnel – but that too had been subject to delays and cost overruns before opening in 1841. But, of course, the original navvies used little more than picks, shovels and the occasional stick of dynamite to cut it. Upgrading railways, just like building them in the first place, is clearly not an exact science.

When Brunel first published his design for the tunnel, few thought it could be built – 1.8 miles long, perfectly straight, and through some challenging geology. More than 100 men lost their lives during the three years of the tunnel's construction. It was even discussed in Parliament, where one MP described the idea as 'dangerous, extraordinary, monstrous and impractical'.

George Stephenson, the great locomotive engineer, is reputed to have said that passengers would be terrified even by the idea of passing through it in a train. Nobody had ever built a tunnel like it before, and yet the great man's achievement is still an essential feature of the GWR line today.

It is said that it is so perfectly straight that on one day each year the rising sun shines right through it: 9 April – Brunel's birthday. Coincidence or just one of Brunel's little

Robert Stephenson's wrought-iron tubular Conwy Railway Bridge – now a Grade I listed historic monument – still carries the North Wales Coast Railway across the River Conwy. Built between 1846 and 1848, it is the last surviving example of this type of bridge. It is seen here from Conwy Castle, with Thomas Telford's suspension bridge – built between 1820 and 1826 – alongside. Both bridges were built using design cues from the castle in the hope of lessening their visual impact on their thirteenth-century neighbour.

A Great Western express leaving the east end of Brunel's 1.8-mile Box Tunnel, *c*. 1910. The arch to the right of the tunnel gave access to the quarries – opened in 1844 – from which much of Bath stone was excavated. The quarry tunnel was later used as a munitions depot during the Second World War, a communications centre during the Cold War, and is now a secure document storage facility.

Above: A London & South Western Railway train leaving London Waterloo station, headed by a 1904-built L12 Class 4-4-0 locomotive, No. 417, designed by Dugald Drummond. From a postcard published *c*. 1910.

Below: The Forth Bridge, as seen from the quayside at North Queensferry. The construction of the bridge was funded by a consortium of the North British Railway, the Midland Railway, the Great Northern Railway and the North Eastern Railway, who collectively raised £3.2 million for the project, reflecting the huge commercial returns which railway entrepreneurs anticipated. That figure would equate with around £400 million today – less than one third of the construction costs of the 2017 Queensferry Crossing cable-stayed road bridge which now crosses the river close by.

The Bridge after accident : Last standing Pier
at North End of Gap

Above right and above left: One of James Valentine's postcards comparing – rather unfairly – one of the piers on the new Tay Bridge with a fragment of a pier from the old. Each span of the old bridge was supported by groups of four of these slender piers (see far right). The 3,286-metre-long Tay Bridge caused particular engineering challenges – the metal superstructure carrying the track can vary in length by over a metre between summer and winter.

gestures to those who doubted that it could ever be done? We will never know. It is certainly precision engineering on a massive scale.

Fifty years later, more than seventy workers died working on Benjamin Baker's Forth Bridge, manufactured and erected by Sir William Arrol & Company. Fourteen men died during the building of Arrol's replacement for Bouch's Tay Bridge between 1883 and 1887, most of them by falling into the river. Two more men died on 12 September 1902 during routine repainting – a sudden squall caused the platform on which they were working to break loose. Eight men had been working on the bridge at the time, causing the *Dundee Evening Telegraph* to comment 'How the others managed to avoid a similar fate is incomprehensible. There were some miraculous escapes.' Maintaining railway tunnels and bridges, it would seem, could be almost as hazardous as building them.

The Forth and Tay bridges were among the last large-scale railway projects undertaken in Victorian Britain. As the nineteenth century was drawing to a close, the railway map was, luckily, virtually complete. 'Luckily', because funds were no longer readily available for such massive capital investments. Many investors in the preceding fifty years had seen the projects which they had been promised would make them rich instead bankrupt a significant number of them.

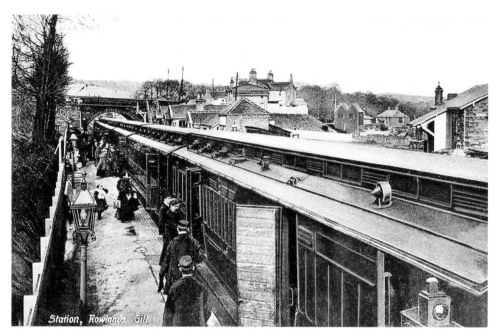

Above: Rowlands Gill station, 6 miles south-west of Gateshead, served the mining village of the same name on the North Eastern Railway's Derwent Valley line. It was opened in 1867. This part of the route was double tracked. In 1914 the line was carrying more than 500,000 passengers per year. By the 1950s coal trains were the main users of the line and, with passenger numbers in decline, Rowlands Gill was one of the stations closed in 1954. The rails were lifted in 1964, the line having closed completely in 1963, and the trackbed is now a walkway and cycle path.

Below: Arriving at Ledbury station, Herefordshire, at the start of the hop-picking season. A 1907 postcard by Tilley & Sons of Ledbury.

A crowded platform at Wimbledon station with passengers awaiting the arrival of the 10 a.m. Up. Bradshaw's Railway Guide for April 1910 lists this train as the 09.43 fast weekday service from Epsom to London Waterloo, stopping at Ewell (09.46) and Worcester Park (09.52). After leaving Wimbledon at precisely 10 a.m., it was scheduled to stop only at Vauxhall (10.11) before arriving at Waterloo at 10.18. Many postcard sales were probably made to people who recognised themselves on the busy platform.

GWR 2021 Class 0-6-0 saddle tank No. 2118, built at Wolverhampton in 1903, is seen here standing at Drybrook Halt in Gloucestershire. The locomotive is hauling a single driving trailer. The caption suggests it was published after the GWR introduced railmotors onto the single-track route in 1908. Even with a steam engine, the train could be operated either from the footplate or from the driving cab at the end of the carriage, thus enabling push-pull operation. The line, originally planned by the Mitcheldean Road & Forest of Dean Railway, opened in 1907. Several light railways also experimented both with push-pull operations and steam railmotors. This is another Tilley & Son postcard.

The main lines did indeed make fortunes for their investors, but one has to wonder at the business plans which suggested that many of the rural lines that were proposed, approved by parliament and constructed at the height of railway-building mania would ever see a recouping of their capital investment, let alone ever make a profit.

Parliamentary scrutiny prior to the passing of each Act of Parliament did look closely at the land acquisition issues, and established standards of both construction and operation, but as it was private money that was being invested, only light scrutiny had been applied at the outset to the probity and financial acumen of the proposing companies and their plans. Unsurprisingly, that led to some investors being seduced by business plans that were quite clearly fraudulent, but it also led to many where the extravagant claims of potential investor benefits were never realistically challenged.

There were, however, strict requirements (by Victorian standards) on the robustness of the trackbed, the gradients, the radius of curves and the loading capacity of bridges if trains were to travel at high speeds. Those rigorous construction standards were expected to be applied to branch lines as well, whether or not trains were ever likely to travel at more than a modest pace.

Such services already operated on existing rural railways across the country – both the GWR and the LNWR had introduced railmotors, or auto-trains, either with a single coach with internal steam or petrol engine, or a steam locomotive and a single driving car, thus avoiding the necessary infrastructure at termini of either a passing loop to run the locomotive around the train, or a turntable. In addition, tramways and mineral lines, as well as narrow gauge railways, were long-established, built to lower construction standards, and yet proven to be safe, reliable and economically viable.

Huge snowdrifts, as a result of the 'Great Snowstorm of 1906', which occurred over three days in late December, completely blocked the line from Dingwall to Kyle of Lochalsh (above). Clearing the track was a major undertaking, with a snow plough attached to the first of three David Jones-designed E Class 'Skye Bogies' built especially for the Dingwall to Skye (Kyle of Lochalsh) route, which had opened just nine years earlier, in 1897. The *Northern Chronicle* carried a report on the blizzard: 'The train going west from Dingwall on Thursday morning got stuck in ten feet of snow near Achterneed Station, about three miles from Dingwall, and it was only after twenty-four hours' hard work that the engine and carriages with the passengers were dug out and taken back to Dingwall early on Friday morning.'

Kyle of Lochalsh station was the terminus of the extension to the Dingwall & Skye Railway from Stromeferry. The Highland Railway had absorbed the Dingwall & Skye Railway in 1880. The line remains open with daily services from Kyle of Lochalsh to Dingwall and Inverness.

Right: Elaborate late Victorian cast ironwork at Sheringham's 1887 station, now the terminus of the North Norfolk Railway.

Below: Although it opened in 1898, two years after the passing of the Light Railways Act, the Lynton & Barnstaple Railway had been authorised by its own Act of Parliament. Thus, despite its operational plans sitting comfortably within the requirements of the new Act, it was built to traditional high standards, the only narrow gauge line to be equipped with full main line signalling.

Lynton and Barnstaple Railway. Blackmoor Gate Station.

A GWR railmotor and driving trailer at Warren Halt near Dawlish, *c.* 1908.

An animated scene at Tan-y-Bwlch station on the narrow gauge Festiniog Railway around 1904. The station was originally opened in 1873, closed in 1939 and reopened in 1958 regulated by the 1896 Light Railways Act. It has gone on to become one of the premier tourist attractions in Wales.

The Dyke station near Brighton was opened in 1887 by the Brighton & Dyke Railway. Trains were operated by the London, Brighton & South Coast Railway. The little branch line had just three stations along its route, and had it not been opened almost a decade before the Light Railways Act was passed, it would have benefitted from the Act's lighter construction requirements. As it was, it was never heavily used, closing for three years between 1917 and 1920, and closing completely in early 1939.

Long after the initial railway bubble had been burst, it became quite clear that if any more railways were ever to be constructed in late Victorian Britain, some way had to be found of streamlining the whole approval process, reducing its often crippling costs and lowering the exacting standards – which for lightly used railways were considerably over-engineered – with which railway builders had to comply.

Trade in late nineteenth-century Britain was booming, causing ever-greater pressure on a patchy and often inadequate road system to move goods to and from railheads. The need to build short feeder railways had long been recognised by the Board of Trade, but under existing legislation the costs involved in such projects – still privately financed, as was the established railway network – rendered them economically impractical.

To resolve the apparent impasse, an innovative piece of legislation was drawn up by the Board of Trade and laid before parliament, embodying some features of a tramway with a lighter version of the construction requirements for traditional railways. It became the Light Railways Act of 1896.

London & North Western Railway's railmotor No. 1 en route between Dysrth and Prestatyn, North Wales, shortly after the service was introduced in 1905. The railway introduced six of these vehicles across several routes. Although the branch line had been established by a separate Act of Parliament in 1869, this was exactly the sort of rural line which the 1896 Light Railways Act was later introduced to encourage.

On the Dyserth Railway, Meliden

The LNWR's push/pull steam railmotor and driving trailer en route between Prestatyn and Dyserth in North Wales. The indecipherable postmark on this Valentine postcard reads 192? – the last digit missing.

The 1896 Light Railways Act

Designed to kick-start a new railway-building era by introducing a streamlined 'fast-track' and lower-cost process for gaining approval for new lines, the 1896 Light Railways Act brought about sweeping changes to the protocols and procedures with which both new and existing railway companies seeking approval for new routes would have to work.

Once the main lines had all been completed, hundreds of branch lines had been laid which brought outlying towns and villages into the network. But as the business cases for later lines became more and more risky, investors baulked at the sheer cost of preparing all the necessary paperwork which preceded any Act of Parliament. As a consequence many of the proposed shorter 'in-fill' routes looked less investable and were shelved. By the 1880s, railway building had almost ground to a halt, despite the fact that many communities still had no railway connections.

And yet, if the costs of preparing the business case and getting legal approval could be pared back, there did seem to be a social as well as a commercial justification for completing some of the rural lines and link lines to broaden access to the network. This was actually an inspired idea, for it was assumed that the sort of lines which might still be constructed would likely only ever have relatively light use, and would not necessarily have to withstand the impact of heavy trains. That meant that many of the robust conditions imposed on the construction of 'traditional' railways – especially in the preparation of the trackbed, construction of bridges, etc. – could be made a little less demanding without compromising safety if only relatively lightweight trains were going to use the lines.

It is worth bearing in mind that in the closing decades of Queen Victoria's reign the road network was still pretty patchy and, and in the days before the ascendency of the motor vehicle, for many it was the train which met their transport needs, both private and commercial. It is also important to remember that while roads and their bridges were funded by public money, the development of railways was still wholly dependent upon private investment. If the initial costs and construction time frames could be reduced, then further expansion of the network might still be of interest to wealthy entrepreneurs.

The concept of 'light railways' had been mentioned in legislation since the 1860s, but neither the Board of Trade nor the increasingly powerful large railway companies had shown much inclination to actively promote the idea. As railway building ground to a near halt as the nineteenth century drew to a close, several influential voices began to try and attract support for the idea – among them local dignitaries who saw the community benefit of being linked to the national network.

Above: A London & South Western Railway Class 02 4-4-2T locomotive, at the head of a five-coach train running through Combpyne Woods towards Lyme Regis in Dorset. The locomotive was designed by William Adams and sixty of the class were built at the LSWR's Nine Elms Works between 1889 and 1895. The LSWR offered through services between Lyme Regis and London Victoria, usually by coupling two branch line coaches to London-bound trains at Axminster, and vice versa. The line was closed in 1965.

Below: Lyme Regis station was opened in 1903 by the Axminster & Lyme Regis Light Railway, a constituent company of the LSWR that had been granted a Light Railway Order in 1899. The railway played a key role in the promotion of the town as an increasingly popular holiday resort. This was exactly the sort of development that the Light Railways Act had been designed to facilitate. Long after the branch line closed, the Lyme Regis station buildings were dismantled in 1979 and rebuilt at Alresford on the Mid-Hants Railway – the Watercress Line.

The light railway was already permitted by both Irish and British railway law, they argued, so why not simplify and encourage their use in mainland Britain? By the early 1890s, support for the idea seemed to be growing with backing from several notable figures. One of those whose support has been credited by railway historians as particularly influential was a London barrister, Major Carne Rasch, then the Member of Parliament for Essex South East, who laid a Bill before Parliament in 1894 seeking to introduce something similar to the Irish light railway regulations into English law.

Robertsbridge Station Sussex

A busy scene at Robertsbridge station on the South Eastern Railway's line between Tunbridge Wells and Hastings, *c.* 1906. Robertsbridge had become a junction just six years earlier with the opening of the Rother Valley Light Railway, later known as the Kent & East Sussex Railway. A K&ESR train can be seen at the left, with a main line train on the adjacent platform. The K&ESR opened to passenger traffic in April 1900, with motive power provided by two William Stroudley-designed ex-London, Brighton & South Coast Railway A1 Class 0-6-0 Terriers built in 1872 and renamed *Bodiam* and *Rolvenden*. Passenger services ended in 1954, but part of the route was reopened as a heritage line in 1974 using its historic name, the K&ESR. *Bodiam*, built as *Poplar*, survives.

The group of dignitaries on the platform may suggest that this postcard marks the first train to arrive at Fort Augustus station – the terminus of the Invergarry & Fort Augustus Railway – in 1903. The locomotive at the head of the train, Highland Railway No. 48, was the ninth and last of the company's 'L' Class 4-4-0 mixed-traffic engines, designed by David Jones and built at the Lochgorm Works between 1882 and 1901. Their use on the Kyle of Lochalsh extension earned them the nickname of 'Skye Bogies'.

Machrihanish Railway, Pier Head Station.

The Campbeltown & Machrihanish Light Railway was a 2-foot 3-inch-gauge line originally built to carry coal. It was granted a Light Railway Order in 1905 and operated passenger services from 1908 until 1932, when it finally yielded to the growing popularity of the bus. The 0-6-2T locomotive *Argyll* was built by Andrew Barclay of Kilmarnock in 1906, the coaches by R. Y. Pickering of Wishaw in 1907.

His proposed device for so doing was to seek Local Authority guarantees for the costs of bringing new light railways into operation – effectively underwriting the construction and operating costs.

It came to nothing, but just a few months later, in early December 1894, the Board of Trade organised a conference to discuss quite similar proposals, and in January 1895 the report of that conference was published – to be met with a mixture of every possible response from strong support to dismissive scorn.

There were understandable debates about passenger safety if the established rigorous standards were lightened, and discussions about what track gauge future light railways would use. One suggestion was that all lines authorised under any proposed new legislation should be narrow gauge – which would have required goods to be loaded and unloaded at any railhead where narrow and standard gauge lines met.

There were many advantages to such a proposal, and among those cited by the advocates of narrow gauge was the belief that such lines could generally be built parallel to existing roads, and therefore result in stations being built at the edges of villages. On many of the branch lines already built, stations were at some considerable distance from villages, often sited there as a result of access difficulties across farmland, or the engineering challenges which would otherwise have been posed by local geology.

The opponents of such an idea – usually the railway companies themselves – justified their opposition by noting the meandering nature of country roads. For their shareholders, the most cost-effective route would always be the most direct one, coming with lower construction costs, shorter distances to be covered and therefore shorter journey times.

Inevitably, the advocates of standard gauge were always going to get their way as they included the large railway companies who saw the revenue-earning potential of local lines feeding into their networks – and were, in any case, going to put up the majority of the money should any such lines ever be built.

A particular suggestion – which the Board of Trade initially opposed – was that goods and passengers could more cost-effectively be carried on combined passenger and freight trains. Hitherto such an arrangement had been vigorously opposed.

When a decision was made to promote a Bill to facilitate the construction of light railways, the legislators fell far short of what might be considered ideal.

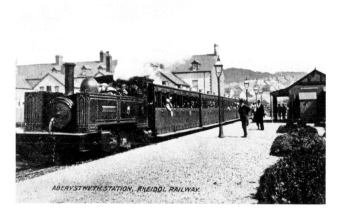

Unlike most preserved railways in Britain, the Vale of Rehidol Railway between Aberystwyth and Devil's Bridge opened under an LRO in 1902 and has operated a steam-hauled continuous service since it was opened – apart from a six-year break during the Second World War. Services were initially hauled by a roster of three locomotives – two 2-6-2T locomotives, built by Davies and Metcalfe, and *Rheidol*, built by Bagnall. The line was taken over by the GWR in 1922, and was then nationalised after the war. In 1968 it became the first part of British Railways to be returned to private ownership.

The Glasgow & South Western Railway introduced steam rail motors onto their Maidens & Dunure Light Railway in 1923, but abandoned the experiment just five years later. The third-class accommodation on the vehicles was not considered sufficiently luxurious for the wealthy and discerning class of passengers making their way from Ayr to Turnberry Hotel and golf course. The world-famous golf course and hotel both owe their existence to the development of the Maidens & Dunure Light Railway, and Turnberry station and the hotel both opened on 17 May 1906, five years after the first thirteen-hole golf course had welcomed its first players. The hotel is now known as the Trump Turnberry.

Nowhere in the proposals was there even a vague definition of what would constitute a light railway, and there was no clear guidance on how such a railway should be built – and even less on how it should be operated. Existing railway law offered little clarification. There was no clear distinction identified between what constituted a 'tramway' as opposed to a 'light railway', and tramways were already subject to the 1870 Tramways Act, which imposed much tighter restrictions on their construction and operation than the proposed light railways regulations.

Despite all these misgivings and ambiguities, the Light Railways Bill was quickly laid before parliament and passed with little or no amendment, and 'an Act to facilitate the Construction of Light Railways in Great Britain' – usually known as the Light Railways Act – became law on 14 August 1896.

A pioneering, if somewhat vague, piece of legislation, it was, however, an important development, as Britain's railways had grown throughout the nineteenth century

A William Stroudley-designed 0-6-0ST tank, No. 56 – built at the Highland Railway's Lochgorm Works in 1869 – prepares to head the first train out of Dornoch station on 2 June 1902. The locomotive *Balnain* was renamed *Dornoch* to mark the occasion. Funding for the new 7.75-mile light railway came from the Duke of Sutherland, the local council and private subscribers. From the outset the line was operated by the Highland Railway, reputedly costing £28,000 to build – around £3 million at today's prices – and continued to run passenger services, often at a loss, until closure in 1960.

Initially proposed as a standard gauge line in 1896 which never managed to raise the required capital support, the Welshpool & Llanfair Railway was granted a Light Railway Order in 1899, opening as a 2-foot 6-inch-gauge line in 1903. Part of the route ran along the streets of Welshpool. Promoted as a means of bringing business to Llanfair, it never made a profit. The 1902-built Beyer-Peacock 0-6-0T locomotives *The Earl* and *Countess* are still running today. Passenger services were withdrawn in 1931, but the route was reopened as a heritage line in 1963.

While most light railways sought to avoid expensive infrastructure such as viaducts, the Invergarry & Fort Augustus Railway had to cross the River Oich to reach Fort Augustus Pier station on Loch Ness. Opened in 1903, minimal public demand for the service saw the line from Fort Augustus to the pier – and the bridge – abandoned in 1906.

without any overarching master plan. Every line that had been built had been approved independently by parliament without any scrutiny as to how each would fit into the development of a coherent national network.

There had, of course, been many Acts of Parliament relating to railways, but with no national master plans, development and duplication of services had been driven not by national need, but purely by commercial competition.

Several Regulation of Railways Acts had been passed since 1840, setting out a range of safety and other requirements – sometimes triggered by events rather than predicting and thus preventing them. Now, for light railways at least, there was an agreed, if somewhat loose, framework within which to proceed, bringing with it hugely reduced costs both in seeking approval for the initial proposal and the actual construction of the line. But nowhere was there a well-articulated definition of what a 'light railway' actually was. Some said that providing such a definition was impossible and that, rather than defining what it was, it would actually be easier to say what it was not.

The architect Sir John Wolfe-Barry – who had recently completed his work on the construction of London's Tower Bridge – suggested they would be little better than the temporary contractors' railways used in the construction of dams, reservoirs and so on.

Above all other considerations, there was a general consensus that passengers could not expect the same comfort and levels of service they were used to if such railways were to be built and operated 'on the cheap'. The mechanisms for gaining approval, however, *were* simplified. Instead of any plans to build a new railway needing specific approval via an Act of Parliament, the new 1896 Act established a small board of just three Light Railway Commissioners who would adjudicate upon each new proposal.

The Commissioners would be appointed by the President of the Board of Trade and, interestingly, their brief was to be proactive and 'to offer, so far as they were able, every facility for considering and maturing proposals to construct light railways'. In other words, they were duty-bound to actively promote the establishment of new lines, rather than just make judgment on proposals laid before them.

It was recognised that the proposals for new routes might come from private companies, local councils or community groups who saw the arrival of a railway as a key to their community's development – or indeed any combination of them.

Local councils were even given the power to authorise loans to the construction companies who would undertake the work. Some councils even saw the potential of such railways to bring new residents and businesses to their communities.

The Act was considered very experimental, and was originally intended to lapse after just five years – presumably giving parliament and the Board of Trade the right to pull the plug on the idea if it didn't work as well as was hoped. In fact, it was not repealed until 1992, when it was superseded by the Transport and Works Act.

Under the Act the costs of such things as the trackbed could be reduced substantially if traffic was limited to three- or four-coach trains running at only moderate speeds and exerting a specified limited weight per axle.

The track foundations and ballasting on main lines, in contrast, had to be able to withstand the weight of express trains running at speed. That, in turn, required track maintenance crews whose daily job was to check, and if necessary re-ballast, the track.

Such a role would not be necessary on the relatively few miles of a light railway where trains would be travelling at a more leisurely pace.

Thus, in addition to the cost savings in construction, operating costs could be substantially reduced, with far fewer employees needed.

Looking more like the type of railway bridge seen in the Wild West, the 1901 trestle bridge at Hardcastle Crags was one of several that formed vital links in the 5.5-mile narrow gauge Blake Dean Light Railway, which was built to facilitate construction of the three dams at Walshaw Dean reservoirs between Hebden Bridge and Top Withins near Halifax in Yorkshire. The railway operated fifteen locomotives, which hauled trains carrying materials while the workers officially travelled on horse-drawn tramcars. The bridge and the railway were dismantled in 1912, five years after the dams were completed.

The Mid-Suffolk Light Railway was one of the most ambitious of those granted LROs. The company initially planned to operate 50 route miles but very quickly ran out of funds. A 19-mile section of the line from Haughley to Laxfield opened to freight in 1904, but it took another four years before passenger traffic was introduced, the trains hauled by Hudswell Clarke 0-6-0T locomotives specially built for the route. Mendlesham Station was opened in September 1908, one of ten stations on the shortened line. All were closed in 1952. A group is currently working towards reopening a section of the line.

The Wigan Light Railway Order, granted on 31 January 1902 after a number of amendments, was one of many relating to trams rather than railways, taking advantage of the 1896 Act's lighter regulation. Approval for the 4-mile route from Poolstock south to Ashton marked the start of the conversion of much of the town's tramway system from narrow gauge to standard gauge. The steam locomotive seen here was built by Kitson & Co. of Airedale Foundry in Leeds. Wigan & District Tramways bought nine of them in the 1890s, and they remained in service until steam was withdrawn from the network in 1903.

Given that most of the routes likely to benefit from the Act would be operated with only one, or at most two trains on the line at any given time, signalling could be reduced – or even eliminated – with trains operating a strict 'staff' or 'token' system.

Level crossings would no longer necessarily need to be gated and station infrastructure could be reduced to a bare minimum. However, crossings remained a perennial concern, as the Act did not identify which took precedence over the other – the existing roadway or the railway passing over it. Several wealthy landowners balked at the cost of building such a railway if, at some time in the future, right of passage over the roadway might be arbitrarily withdrawn. None of these things, however, are specifically mentioned in the Act of Parliament. It would seem that the Light Railway Commissioners and their Railway Inspectors had the authority to reach their decisions on such matter on an individual basis.

Axle load and maximum running speed are not enshrined in the Act itself – contrary to many published sources. Rather, they are contained within other earlier legislation with which light railway operators were bound to comply – and those existing Acts were listed in the 1896 legislation. The Act ran to fifteen pages, but contained little detail about what would constitute a light railway. The key section was the 'Second Schedule' on the penultimate page, sub-headed 'Enactments Relating to Safety, &c.', which referenced sections from earlier applicable legislation, namely: '2 & 3 Vict. c.45. An Act to amend an Act of the fifth and sixth years of the reign of his late Majesty King William the Fourth relating to highways' (the whole Act); '5 & 6 Vict. c.55 The Railway Regulations Act, 1842' (sections four, five, six, nine, and ten); '9 & 10 Vict. c.57 An Act for regulating the gauge of railways' (the whole Act); '31 & 32 Vict. c.119 The Regulation of Railways Act 1868' (sections nineteen, twenty, twenty-two, twenty-seven, twenty-eight and twenty-nine); '34 & 35 Vict. c.78 The Regulation of Railways Act 1871' (the whole Act); '36 & 37 Vict. c.76 The Railway Regulation Act (Returns of signal arrangements, working, &c.), 1873' (sections four and six); '41 & 42 Vict. c.20 The Railways Returns (Continuous Brakes) Act 1878' (the whole Act); '46 & 47 Vict. c.34 The Cheap Trains Act 1883' (section three); and '52 & 53 Vict. c.57 The Regulation of Railways Act 1889' (the whole Act).

Originally opened in 1865, and saved in 1951 by the Talyllyn Railway Preservation Society, the narrow gauge line – seen here in an Edwardian postcard – became the first in the world to be operated by enthusiasts.

Key among those was the Regulation of Railways Act of 1868, which contained a lot of the operational detail that the 1896 Act omitted. Sections 27, 28 and 29 of that Act referred specifically to light railways – and also hinted at a loosening of construction and operational requirements which would eventually be embodied in the 1896 Act.

Clause 27 of the 1868 Act stated that 'The Board of Trade may by Licence authorize a Company applying for it to construct and work or to work as a Light Railway the whole or any Part of a Railway which the Company has the Power to construct or work.'

Of course while the construction standards required for such a railway may have been less rigorous than conventional lines, the approval process was still lengthy, albeit without the expense of an Act of Parliament. Given that possibility, why some companies still elected to go through the fully parliamentary process is surprising.

Clause 28 contained the important detail, defining a maximum weight per axle of just 8 tons and a maximum permitted speed of 25 mph – therefore those restrictions, while often erroneously attributed to the 1896 Act, predate it by more than three decades.

But, back to the 1868 Act. The associated 'Conditions and Regulations for Light Railways' promised severe penalties for any operator breaching those conditions, threatening 'any such Person on Conviction on Indictment for any Offence relating to the Weight of Engines, Carriages, or Vehicles, or the Speed of Trains, shall be also liable to Imprisonment, with or without Hard Labour, for any Term not exceeding Two Years'. But, despite all the almost-threatening language concerning breaches of some of regulations contained in many of the existing Acts of Parliament, it appears that individual Board of Trade inspectors had long had a measure of discretion over how rigorously the regulations were implemented and policed. As an example, they appear to have exercised the right to override some aspects of the Railway Returns (Continuous Brakes) Act of 1878 when it came to mixed-traffic trains on lightly used lines.

It was not an entirely level playing field and it made sense to have an Act specifically related to light railways and to vest that discretion in a small group of decision makers. The 1896 Act can therefore be seen as an attempt to further simplify existing procedures for seeking approval to operate a light railway – a Light Railway Order replacing the Board of Trade Licence specified in 1868.

After the passing of the 1896 Act, early signs were promising; some lines which had been mooted in the 1850s and 1860s but never built – because of cost, a lack of investors, or lack of a viable business plan – did actually come to fruition.

The first to take advantage of the 'lighter' touch regulations was the Basingstoke & Alton Light Railway, which was granted a Light Railway Order on 9 December 1897 – the first of four such approvals in the first year. It was certainly not the success its backers had anticipated, and the track was reportedly lifted in 1917 – only to be relaid in 1924 after protests from farmers. It survived only until 1936.

Within the first three years of the Act being passed into law, there were no fewer than 175 applications for Light Railway Orders and almost all of the proposals were for standard gauge lines. In the end the Act had not specified any approved gauge, so a small number of narrow gauge routes were also constructed under LROs.

One standard gauge line, the Lauder Railway, had originally been proposed back in 1852, connecting the small town of Lauder with the Waverley Route to Edinburgh. Despite initial public enthusiasm locally, the project had been abandoned. The idea was revived and abandoned again in both the 1870s and the 1880s, but with the introduction of the Light Railways Act it was revisited once again. With the support of two local landowners – the Marquis of Tweeddale and the Earl of Lauderdale – this time matters progressed, and after further delays a Light Railway Order was granted in 1898, and initial planning and surveying work was started.

The successful proposal embodied many of the aspirations of the Board of Trade officials who had drawn up the Act. The project was to be a partnership between Dick Kerr & Company, who would build it and partially finance it – taking shares in the railway as part payment – along with Berwickshire County Council and the North British Railway, who would also operate services on the line using a pair of ageing Dugald Drummond-designed R Class 0-6-0 tank engines in return for 40 per cent of gross takings on both passengers and goods.

Construction work started on the permanent way when the first sod was cut by the Countess of Lauderdale on 3 June 1899 and it took two years to complete the 10.5-mile route between Lauder and Fountainhall Junction, with a single intermediate station at Oxton.

Kilmarnock-based Dick, Kerr & Company had a long history of involvement in the construction of tramways – including steam tram engines – so the engineering freedoms and constraints implicit in the new rules would not have been entirely new to them.

When it started passenger operations on 2 July 1901, the Lauder Light Railway was the first new line to be opened in Scotland in the twentieth century, and the first under the jurisdiction of the new legislation. The 10.5-mile journey took just over three-quarters of an hour, leading one newspaper to report that: 'The speed of the railway is perhaps not quite in harmony with the rush and hurry of the age.'

It was not the first in Scotland to be granted approval, however – that was the Bankfoot Light Railway. Just 3 miles in length from Strathord Junction on the Caledonian Railway to Bankfoot, it initially made a small operating profit, but not enough to suggest that its £38,000 construction costs could quickly be recouped.

It had been the subject of two separate LROs before building work started, the first in 1898 and a second – technically an enabling order giving its backers an extension of time to get it completed – in 1903. Most LROs specified a period of time within which funding had to be raised and work commenced. The railway did not remain independent for long,

Lauder station was the terminus of the Lauder Light Railway, running from Fountainhall Junction on the Waverley Route to the village of Lauder, which opened in 1901. The line was closed in 1932 with the Waverley Route itself closing in 1961. The locomotive approaching the station is a Class R 4-4-0T, designed for the NBR by Dugald Drummond and built at their Cowlairs Works in the early 1880s.

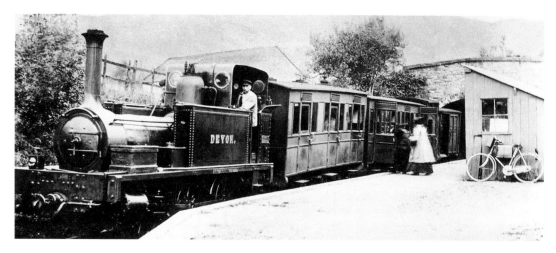

The 3-foot-gauge Ravenglass & Eskdale Railway
in Cumbria was originally opened in 1875 to carry
haematite from mines near Boot to the Furness
Railway's main line at Eskdale. It gained approval to
run passenger services the following year using a pair
of new Manning Wardle 0-6-0T locomotives – *Devon*
(top) and *Nabb Gill* (above). *Devon* was delivered in
1876, *Nabb Gill* in 1877. These views date from 1905–10.
By 1913 the line had been closed. It reopened two years
later in 1915, re-laid to 15-inch gauge by Wenman
Joseph Bassett-Lowke – he of model locomotive
fame – having been granted a Light Railway Order.
It still operates today. The 2-6-2 locomotive *Northern
Rock* (left) was built in-house and had just entered
service when this picture was taken in 1976.

The Southwold Railway in Suffolk, which opened in 1879, was one of several narrow gauge lines that had been authorised as a Light Railway under the 1868 Regulation of Railways Act. The 8.75-mile, 3-foot-gauge line from Southwold to Halesworth initially operated three 2-4-0T locomotives built by Sharp, Stewart & Co. of Manchester. In 1893, the Sharp Stewart 2-4-2T *Southwold*, seen here, replaced an earlier locomotive of the same name. Light Railway Orders under the 1896 Act were granted in 1907 authorising the railway to build extensions – one to Southwold Harbour the other to Lowestoft – but they were never constructed. The decision to close the line in 1929 took the local merchants who used it to transport their produce completely by surprise – so much so that the closure had to be delayed by ten days to clear the backlog of freight already booked in for transport. The upper image is one of an extensive series of cards showing life on the railway, produced before 1920, while the lower card was published by local photographer F. Jenkins to mark the line's demise. The track and locomotives were eventually broken up for scrap in 1941.

SOUTHWOLD RAILWAY TRAIN. SEP 1879 - APRIL 1929.

however, being absorbed by the Caledonian Railway after less than three years. Passenger services lasted only twenty-five years, and goods services were withdrawn in 1964.

The Leadhills & Wanlockhead Railway – a Caley branch line from the outset – was partially opened in 1901, opening fully in 1902. Part of the route is still used by a 2-foot-gauge tourist line today.

Within the Act's original intended lifetime of five years – a considerable number of new lines having been proposed, and with obvious interest being shown by numerous other groups – the Board of Trade commissioners took the decision to ask parliament to extend the regulations. However, that five-year period was not long enough for the approved lines to be built and commissioned, and many of them never would be.

In August 1901 alone – the year the decision to extend the life of the Act was enabled – the Board of Trade notified parliament that four new Light Railway Orders had been granted in Lancashire alone: the Blackpool & Garstang Light Railway Order, the Nelson Light Railway Order, the Barrowford Light Railway Order, and the Colne & Trawden Light Railway Order. The Central Essex Light Railway Order had also been approved while, in Yorkshire, the Tickhill Light Railway Order and the Wales & Laughton Light Railway Order had both been granted after Board of Trade modifications. The Bridlington & North Frodingham Light Railway Order of 1898 was also approved with amendments.

The Tickhill Light Railway was planned to run between Haxey in North Lincolnshire and Tickhill, south of Doncaster – a distance of 8 miles – but the line was never completed, getting only as far as Bawtry, to the east of Tickhill, and with no connections with any of the three major railway companies in the area: the GNR, the GCR, and the L&YR.

It remained independent for just six years, being taken over by the GNR in 1907 before construction work on the route had even been started. It eventually opened for goods traffic between Haxey and Bawtry in 1912, but it was said to have lasted just a few years before part of the track was lifted.

LROs saw several other short lengths of line opened in Yorkshire, most notably the Humber Commercial Railway & Dock Company's line from Ulceby near New Holland to Immingham. Granted its LRO in 1904, the company eventually ran its first train in 1910, connecting with the Grimsby District Light Railway which had been built by the GCR and which also opened for freight traffic in 1910. From 1911 it also established connections with the Barton & Immingham Light Railway, which had been authorised in 1907 and was absorbed by the HCR&D in 1912.

Hansard also reported that the Commissioners, confirmed by the Board of Trade, had approved amendments to the Great Western Railway (Pewsey and Salisbury) Light Railway Order, 1898, and the Pewsey & Salisbury (Devizes Branch) Light Railway Order, 1898, Pewsey & Salisbury Light Railway (Extension of Time) Order, 1901.

That same parliamentary submission granted an extension to the Lizard Light Railway (Extension of Time) Order, effectively giving its backers more time to raise funds and construct the line. The Bridlington and North Frodingham Light Railway (Extension of Time) Order did the same. For the Lizard Extension, however, extra time did not improve the railway's ability to raise funds, and the plan was abandoned.

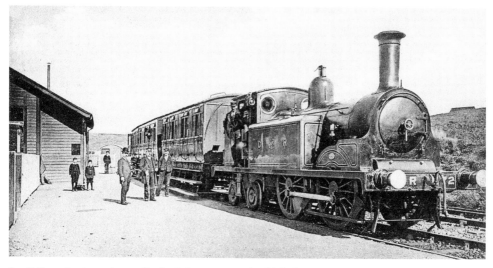

Leadhills station in south-west Scotland, from a postcard published shortly after the Leadhills & Wanlockhead Light Railway was fully opened in 1902. The route was operated from the outset by the Caledonian Railway. When the first phase of the line was opened in 1901, Leadhills became the highest standard gauge station in Britain – a claim to fame it lost just a year later when the line was completed to Wanlockhead. The Dugald Drummond Class 171 0-4-4T No. 172 – built at the Caley's St Rollox Works in Glasgow in 1884 – was the first to work the line.

Building the Calstock Viaduct across the Tamar on the Bere Alston & Calstock Railway was a major undertaking. Work started in 1904 and was completed in 1907. Its most innovative feature was a 113-feet-high steam-powered lift – the red structure in this 1908 postcard – which was used to raise and lower wagons from the railway to the quayside below. The lift was decommissioned in 1934. The twelve-arch viaduct itself was built of pre-cast concrete blocks, manufactured in a makeshift factory on-site.

The Bere Alston & Calstock Railway, which had been upgraded from narrow gauge to standard gauge, was granted a Light Railway Order in March 1900, but it took eight years before passenger services started in March 1908 when the company ran its first trains on the 4-mile branch line from Bere Alston to Callington Road – a line which turned out to be the south-west region's last new opening during the Edwardian era.

The new line was the subject of a lengthy report in the *Western Daily Mercury,* which reported: 'What has not unfairly been described as one of the most charming sections of railway line in the kingdom was opened for passenger traffic yesterday. It is to be known as the Plymouth Devonport, and South Western Junction Railway, or, alternatively, as the Bere Alston & Calstock Light Railway.'

The branch line did not survive the Beeching axe and part of it was eventually closed in 1966. As it was, reportedly, a beautiful route to travel, had it survived, it might possibly have become a popular heritage line by now.

Many more were reported in the pages of *Hansard,* and with that level of interest it must have seemed that the Light Railways Act was going to fulfil its promise. By 1905, however, new applications were down to just two or three per year. Indeed, the majority of the light railways for which approval had been granted would never be built, but throughout the years of the Act, around 550 miles of new lines *were* opened.

Another 300 miles of existing tramways were converted to light railways, taking advantage of the lighter regulation which the Act permitted. That was definitely *not* what those who had advocated the 1896 Act intended to happen – the Light Railways Act had specifically been intended to enable railways to be developed in rural areas to promote the flow of agricultural produce and other locally produced goods.

Some lines, which had been authorised via the conventional parliamentary process but had subsequently hit hard times, were 'reinvented' as light railways during the years leading up to the outbreak of the First World War. Among them was the

Shropshire & Montgomeryshire Railway, one of a group of light railways now often collectively referred to as 'Colonel Stephens' Railways'.

Colonel Holman Stephens was a staunch advocate of the light railway and a great believer in the benefits that such railways and tramways could bring to rural areas. In total he was involved in constructing or managing sixteen lines. Among them was the Rother Valley Railway, which later became the Kent & East Sussex Railway and was almost certainly the first new line built under the 1896 Act to carry fare-paying passengers, opening for service in 1900. Fittingly, opposite the heritage Kent & East Sussex Railway's station at Tenterden is the Colonel Stephens Railway Museum, dedicated to the history and achievements of the man himself.

Taking pride of place in the museum is the Shropshire & Montgomeryshire Railway's locomotive *Gazelle*, on loan from the NRM in York, and described as the smallest preserved standard gauge locomotive in the world. Built in 1893 by A. Dodman & Co. Ltd at their Highgate Works in King's Lynn, the 2-2-2 well-tank locomotive was bought by Stephens in 1911, rebuilt as an 0-4-2 and used to pull the inspection train on the Shropshire & Montgomeryshire Railway, which he had saved from dereliction.

LROs were granted, enabling the construction of the Amesbury & Military Camp Light Railway, the first on 14 September 1897 and a 2.75-mile extension order to Bulford on 10 January 1903. Bulford Camp had opened in 1897. The line ran 13.5 miles from the LSWR's main line near Newton Tony in Wiltshire, through Amesbury and on to Bulford. Passenger services ended in 1952 but military trains continued until 1963.

The Great North of Scotland Railway's Fraserburgh station was also the terminus of the 4.5-mile Fraserburgh & St Combs Light Railway, which was granted its LRO in September 1899 and opened in 1903. The branch line train to the right of this postcard *c.* 1910 is GNSR No. 8, a James Manson-designed Class D 0-6-0T (later LNER J90 Class) built in Leeds in 1885 by Kitson & Company.

The S&MR had originally been opened in stages from 1864 as the Shrewsbury & North Wales Railway – later the Potteries, Shrewsbury & North Wales Railway – but the line had always been disastrously short of money and closed in 1880. Stephens first tried to revive the route in 1905, eventually being granted an LRO in 1910. Trains started operating passenger services again in 1911, initially with promising results, but they were abandoned again in 1933, part of the route becoming a military railway in 1941.

One of Colonel Stephens' later undertakings was the Ashover Light Railway, for which he acted as engineer. Originally planned as a standard gauge line, an LRO was granted in 1919, but by 1921, when an extension was mooted, the decision was made to convert the line to 2-foot gauge and run ex-War Department, American-built Baldwin locomotives. A new LRO backing this proposal was granted in 1922, with a further extension approved in 1924.

These were conditional on passenger services as well as the mineral trains to and from the Clay Cross Company's works and quarries, for which the line had originally been planned. By 1950, however, and by then with only one employee, the line was closed, the track being lifted shortly afterwards.

Midsomer Norton station, closed in 1966, has been restored by the Somerset & Dorset Railway Heritage Trust, who now operate a short length of track under a Light Railway Order.

The Shropshire & Montgomeryshire Railway's Llanymynech station, in the village of the same name on the Shropshire/Powys border, shortly after it was reopened in 1911 by Colonel Stephens, the line having been granted a Light Railway Order in 1910.

Above: The standard gauge Cleobury Mortimer & Ditton Priors Light Railway in Shropshire was granted a Light Railway Order in March 1901, but it would be seven years before the line opened. The 12-mile route ran from the Great Western's Wyre Forest Line at Cleobury Mortimer to Ditton Priors. Planned extensions to Bridgnorth and Coalport were never built. Early locomotives included two 0-6-0ST Manning Wardle saddle tanks, one of which can be seen in this photograph *c.* 1920. Absorbed by the GWR in 1923, in 1938 it was taken over by the Royal Navy to maintain access to their arms depot at Ditton Priors. The engineer was Everard Calthorp, better known for designing narrow gauge lines, among them the Leek & Manifold Vallery Light Railway, also in Shropshire.

Below: The standard gauge Bideford, Westward Ho! & Appledore Railway had been operational for three years before it applied for an LRO in 1904, to permit it to construct a 1.5-mile extension to Appledore. The line was opened in stages between 1901 and 1908, with two-coach trains hauled by one of three Hunslet 2-4-2T locomotives – called *Grenville*, *Kingsway* and *Torridge*, with part of the line running along the street in Bideford down to the quayside. The three pairs of coaches were built at the Bristol Coach & Carriage Works Company, who had also built vehicles for the narrow gauge Festiniog and Lynton & Barnstaple railways. Trains were initially permitted to run at up to 40 mph on the rural sections of the route, reducing to just 4 mph on the streets of Bideford. The line was commandeered for military purposes in 1917 and never reopened for public use after the war had ended.

More than 300 light railway orders – or modifications and extensions to orders – were approved by the Board of Trade Light Railway Commissioners between 1896 and the end of the Great War, but fewer than a quarter of them ever got beyond the planning stage. Despite the considerably reduced set-up costs made possible by the relaxed construction benchmarks permitted by the 1896 Act, the working capital necessary to build and operate many of the proposed lines proved impossible to attract.

The closing years of the nineteenth century saw the introduction of massive changes in transport in Britain, not least of which was the advent of the road vehicle – the far-reaching impact of which it had on the railways could never have been fully anticipated.

A glimpse of things to come, nationally? The busy scene outside Helston station, from a postcard published after the GWR started operating motor buses on the 11-mile route by road from Helston to the Lizard, thus saving the estimated £85,000 cost of building the light railway extension. The cheaper option of running buses instead of trains predated Dr Beeching by more than half a century. The belief that buses could replace trains without loss of passenger amenity was a tenet of his proposals.

In the same year that the Light Railways Act became law, the Locomotives on Highways Act was also passed, removing the need for a man with a red flag to walk in front of a traction engine or steam lorry, while at the same time raising the speed limits on roads to 12 mph. The timing could not have been worse, heralding as it did the start of a dramatic rise in the numbers of road vehicles.

Thus, while the Light Railways Act sought to encourage the building of new railways, the Locomotives on Highways Act made the shipment of goods by road a much more economically viable prospect. While railways could deliver goods quickly and efficiently from station to station, stations were often well outside the communities they served.

This was the start of another transport revolution; indeed, the number of people who attended the very first Motor Show at the Imperial Institute in London that same year was a clear demonstration that the motor vehicle was the future.

As a consequence, some sort of additional transport was necessary to complete the journey from station to factory and vice versa. Steam, and later petrol, road vehicles could deliver those same goods from door to door without using the railway at all, and often undercutting freight charges as well.

An early casualty was the proposed 11.25-mile extension to the Helston Railway intended to extend it to the Lizard, which was first granted an LRO in 1897. An extension to that order was granted in July 1901, but in the end the GWR – which had recently acquired the company – elected to abandon the costs of laying the railway and instead introduce 16 hp Milnes-Daimler single-deck motor buses in 1903.

The 1896 Light Railways Act had, quite simply, arrived too late – how much more effective might such a law have been had it been enacted in the 1860s rather than the 1890s as the age of steam and motor road vehicles dawned? But the 'unintended consequences' of the Act remaining on the statute books would prove to be far-reaching. Its impact has been much greater in the last sixty years than in its first sixty.

The Unintended Consequences

What we now think of as the indecent haste with which lines closed by British Railways in the 1960s were ripped up and relatively new steam locomotives were sent to the breakers' yard is a point of view only possible with the benefit of hindsight. Britain's railways following the Second World War were dirty, old fashioned and often unpleasant to travel on. Nostalgia for steam traction and a delight at being hauled by a steam engine was, for all but a few people, still a thing of the future – the old adage that we never actually miss something until it is gone turned out to be very true.

I well remember the routine that was a regular feature of us setting off on holiday in the late 1950s – travelling from Stirling to Crail on the Fife coast, part of the journey in corridor-less compartment coaches. Our 'holiday luggage' would have been sent on in a large trunk a couple of days before us and would have been delivered to our holiday house before we got there, while we children would travel in clothes which had seen better days. We would not wear them again until the return journey, our clean clothes being saved for the holiday itself.

Left and opposite: By the early 1970s, scrapyards across Britain were already full of abandoned rusting locomotives, but soon all that would change; Photographed in 1980, inside the cab of ex-LMS 4-6-0 Jubilee No. 45699 *Galatea*, still lying in a scrapyard fifteen years after being withdrawn from service and stripped of anything which could be salvaged for reuse in other restoration projects; One of *Galatea*'s driving wheels, cut in 1970/71 – some sources suggest that was to render it beyond restoration. They were wrong; The yard at the Scottish Railway Preservation Society's newly formed Bo'ness & Kinneil Railway in Scotland in 1980; A rusting locomotive and coach await restoration in Haverthwaite Tunnel on what would become the Lakeside & Haverthwaite Railway.

A few years later as a student in the early 1960s, I regularly travelled from Stirling to Manchester at the start and end of each term, invariably on a train hauled by a Stanier Black 5, or a BR Standard Class 5, as far as Preston, stopping at Beatock and Tebay for banker engines to be coupled up for the long haul up and over Beatock and Shap summits. As a keen photographer – albeit with very limited funds to spend on film back then – I always meant to photograph them working hard up those inclines, but somehow never really got around to it.

And then they were all gone, the rhythm of the steam engine replaced by the low thrum of a diesel. 'Modern' rail travel was clean and relatively reliable in the early days

Former GWR Class 57XX 0-6-0PT No. 9629, built at Swindon in 1945 and awaiting cosmetic restoration shortly after its arrival at Carnforth, Lancashire, in 1981. No. 9629 is now being restored at the Pontypool & Blaenavon Railway in South Wales. The GWR built a total of 863 of these locomotives.

LMS Jubilee Class 4-6-0 No. 5690 *Leander* – built at Crewe in 1936 and withdrawn thirty years later – was retrieved from Barry scrapyard in 1972 and restored in Derby by the Leander Locomotive Society. This photograph was taken at Bridgnorth on the Severn Valley Railway in the 1990s. *Leander* is now shedded at West Coast Railways in Carnforth.

Above left: The Great Northern Railway's logo on the former King's Cross footbridge, re-erected over the track and yards at Ropley on the Watercress Line. The cast-iron and wrought-iron bridge had been manufactured for the NER by Andrew Handyside & Co. Ltd of Derby and London, and erected over the platforms in the main train shed in 1892.

Above right: Aboyne station, photographed in June 1972, was originally opened in 1859 by the Aboyne & Ballater Railway. The company later became part of the Great North of Scotland Railway. Both line and station were closed in 1966.

Above left: A derelict GWR 57XX Class 0-6-0PT provisionally earmarked for the Plym Valley Railway near Plymouth and requiring a great deal of work before it could ever be returned to steam. Photographed in the early 1980s.

Above right: Before moving to its present site at Bury, the East Lancashire Railway stored a number of its locomotives just outside Helmshore station in the 1970s.

Below: Britain's love of steam trains brings crowds out wherever they run. Here, BR Standard Class 4 2-6-4T No. 80104, built at Brighton in 1955, draws crowds as it pulls into Swanage station in August 2018. No. 80104 lay in the Barry scrapyard for eighteen years before being rescued in 1984. Rebuilt, it entered service on the Swanage Railway in 1997.

Riding on the footplate of
No.7827 *Lydham Manor*
on the Dartmouth Steam
Railway. The locomotive,
built to GWR 7800 Class
specification, was completed
in December 1950, so the
GWR livery it carried for
many years in preservation
was incorrect. It was sent to
Woodham Brothers in 1966,
was rescued in 1970, and
returned to steam in 1973. It is
now painted in BR black.

West Country Class
No. 34092 *City of Wells*
engulfed in a cloud of steam
at Oxenhope station on the
Keighley & Worth Valley
Railway in the 1990s. The
locomotive has since moved
to the East Lancashire
Railway.

BR Standard Class 7 No. 70000 *Britannia* waits for the
signal to change. The first of a class of fifty-five designed
by Robert Riddles, *Britannia* was built at Crewe in 1951
and withdrawn in 1966. Immediately stored for future
preservation, the locomotive escaped the indignity of
spending years in a breakers' yard. This photograph
was taken at the Steamtown Museum in Carnforth,
Lancashire, in the 1990s. Steamtown had been granted
a Light Railway Order to operate trains over its short
length of track in 1973. Now the headquarters of the
West Coast Railway Company, the Grade II* listed 1930s
and 1940s buildings at Carnforth – including coaling
towers (see page 23), ash pits and locomotive sheds – are
now on Historic England's 'Heritage at Risk' list.

Above: Firing ex-BR 9F No. 92203 *Black Prince* on the North Norfolk Railway, 2016. The locomotive was purchased direct from British Railways for £3,000 by the railway and wildlife artist David Shepherd in 1967. Shepherd gave it its name, and he operated it for many years on his East Somerset Railway.

Right: Robert Stephenson & Hawthorn's 0-6-0ST *Moorbarrow* at Cranmore station on the East Somerset Railway in 2013. The 1955-built former NCB locomotive is now at the Gwili Railway in Wales.

Poor old Dr Beeching – whose report was as logical as it was ruthless, as rational as it was flawed – got the blame for taking a dispassionate look at a system comprising large parts that were no longer fit for purpose.

The Beeching Plan was rational in as much that many routes were uneconomic; ruthless in that his brief did not accept that railways were an important and sometimes essential service for those with no access to cars or buses. It was logical in so much that he had been given the task of attempting to make railways pay their way – or at least reduce the considerable losses they were making – but flawed in cutting large areas of the country out of railway access completely.

With the rise in car ownership, hundreds of trains were being used by only handfuls of passengers, and Ernest Marples, then Minister of Transport, made little or no effort to conceal his preference for creating a modern motorway network rather than invest in railways.

1924-built GWR 4500 Class 2-6-2T Small Prairie No. 4561 spent thirteen years in Barry scrapyard before being rescued by the West Somerset Railway, eventually being returned to steam in 1989. This photograph was taken at Bishops Lydeard in 1991. The locomotive is currently nearing the end of a £250,000 restoration, aimed at returning it to steam once again in 2019.

Left: *Salmon*, an 0-6-0ST locomotive built in 1942 by Andrew Barclay at Kilmarnock, seen here on the Swindon & Cricklade Railway in 2010, is now a regular sight on the Royal Deeside Railway at Crathes, Kincardineshire.

Below: Ex-Southern Railways Bulleid Pacific No. 35005 *Canadian Pacific* was yet another locomotive rescued from Woodhams and restored. Seen here running round the train at Rawtenstall during a visit to the East Lancashire Railway in the early 1990s, No. 35005 is currently undergoing a major overhaul at Eastleigh before returning home to the Watercress Line.

The demise of rural railways was hastened by timetabling changes, which meant that many local trains no longer connected with main line services, further reducing demand. There were those who saw such changes as wilful rather than simple incompetence.

Huge numbers of locomotives were rendered surplus to requirements and over the following five years they, along with thousands of miles of track, were consigned to scrapyards, to eventually be recycled.

The idea of preserving important pieces of railway ephemera was nothing new however – historic locomotives had been being saved and restored throughout the twentieth century. Even the private railway companies had seen the merit in preserving some of their iconic equipment in the years before nationalisation. Stephenson's *Locomotion* was the first, its historical importance being recognised as early as 1875.

The Liverpool & Manchester Railway's 0-4-2 locomotive No. 57 *Lion* spent many years after its railway service was over being used as a static engine driving a pump in Liverpool Docks before being saved and restored in the 1930s.

Lion later went on to have a starring role in the 1953 Ealing comedy *The Titfield Thunderbolt*, in many ways predicting the establishment of enthusiast-operated standard gauge lines long before Dr Beeching came onto the scene.

Lion also played an active role during 'Rocket 150', the 150th anniversary of the famous Rainhill Trials celebrated in May 1980 along the same length of the Liverpool & Manchester Railway's track, and while it was replicas of both *Rocket* and *Sans Pareil* which took part, *Lion* was the oldest original locomotive to steam in the cavalcade by some measure. The locomotive is now displayed in the Museum of Liverpool.

Above left: 0-4-2 *Lion*, built in 1838 for the Liverpool & Manchester Railway, in steam at the 150th anniversary of the Rainhill Trials in 1980.

Above right: William Stroudley's 0-4-2 locomotive *Gladstone* at York's National Railway Museum. It was built in 1882 for the London, Brighton & South Coast Railway and was withdrawn in 1927, when it was bought by the Stephenson Locomotive Society and restored.

The Stephenson Locomotive Society, which was instrumental in saving and restoring the LB&SCR's *Gladstone* – now displayed at the head of Queen Victoria's Royal Train at the National Railway Museum in York – was actually established as far back as 1909.

So, while recognising that early locomotives were an important part of our heritage and should be preserved, preserving and operating an actual railway would be a challenge of a completely different order, with many legal, health and safety, and insurance ramifications. While many routes immediately disappeared from the timetables, some would soon be offered a future by the unexpected consequence of that 1896 Act which had never been repealed.

The fireman of ex-GWR *Hinton Manor* handing over the token at Hampton Loade Station on the Severn Valley Railway in the 1990s. Each token is unique to the section of track which it gives the train and its crew authority to enter. The use of the token system was one of the safety features recommended for use on light railways, reducing the requirement for expensive signalling, although today's heritage lines use traditional signalling as well.

Above: BR Standard Class 4 No. 76079 at the East Lancashire Railway in 1993 just after the locomotive had been given the name *Trevor T. Jones* after the ELR's chairman. The name was removed when No. 76079 was bought by the North Yorkshire Moors Railway, where it operates today.

Left: The driver of Caledonian Railway McIntosh Class 439 0-4-4T No. 419 receiving the token at Kinneil Halt on the Bo'ness & Kinneil Railway in the 1980s. Built at St Rollox Works in Glasgow in 1907, No. 419 is now the 'flagship' of the Scottish Railway Preservation Society's collection, and returned to steam in 2018 after a major overhaul.

Above left: Designed by Samuel Johnson and built in Derby for the Midland Railway in 1880, this Class 1377 locomotive was reclassified as 1F and given the British Railways number 41708 in 1949. Seen at Swanage station in the early 1990s, the locomotive us currently based at Barrow Hill and is awaiting a major overhaul.

Above right: Ex-BR 4MT No. 76084, another locomotive rescued from Barry, was returned to service on the North Norfolk Railway in 2013 after sixteen years of restoration work.

Photographed in 1975, Nos 45212 and 5025 are seen in steam outside Haworth sheds on the Keighley & Worth Valley Railway, which celebrated fifty years as a heritage line in 2018. 45212 had hauled the penultimate scheduled steam-hauled passenger service on British Railways – the 8.50 p.m. service from Preston to Blackpool on 3 August 1968.

The idea of enthusiasts taking over and running railways can be traced back to the closure of the narrow gauge Southwold Railway in Suffolk in 1929 – a closure which was immediately followed by an attempt by a group of locals to get backing to reopen it. Sadly, they failed.

Twenty years later, a group was formed to try and take over the loss-making Talyllyn Railway. They were successful, their task made a little simpler by the fact that the narrow gauge route already operated under light railway conditions, and was already operated by a private company rather than a nationalised monolith.

Above and right: Southern Railways 1934-built Schools Class 4-4-0 *Cheltenham* at Alresford – also on the Watercress Line. There are only three survivors of the forty Schools Class locos built – the others are *Repton* on the North Yorkshire Moors Railway and *Stowe* on the Bluebell.

Opposite: 1959-built 9F 2-10-0 No. 92212 undergoing a few running repairs at Ropley yard on the Mid-Hants Railway – the Watercress Line – in August 2018.

The railway thus became the world's first enthusiast-operated heritage line. Thankfully, over the years the challenge of bringing railways back to life has been enthusiastically embraced by a large number of preservation groups, and the scale of their achievements so far surpasses anything which might have been thought possible fifty years ago.

While narrow gauge lines proved challenging enough, it was anything but a straightforward task to reopen a standard gauge railway, operating regulations being mired in a century and more of railway legislation, all still on the statute books. Luckily a supportive camaraderie quickly evolved among volunteer groups

The first two standard gauge lines to get off the mark were the Middleton Railway in Leeds and the Bluebell Railway – the latter a direct result of British Railways' decision to close the Lewes to East Grinstead line in Sussex in 1954 amidst a great deal of acrimonious local protest. The line was closed, reopened again, and then finally closed in 1958. Just a year later, four local teenagers established the Lewes & East Grinstead Railway Preservation Society and they managed to persuade BR to lease a section of the line to their newly formed limited operating company. With BR's assistance, a Light Railway Order was obtained, rights transferred to the new company, and trains started running again – initially just at weekends – in 1960.

That was the year in which the Middleton Railway Preservation Society was formed, largely by Leeds University students. Their success, and the success of all the others operating today, has been made possible thanks to the simple fact that the 1896 Light Railways Act was still on the statute books. Without it, arguably, the reopening of the heritage lines which we enjoy today would not have been possible.

And yet, the original purpose of the Act – which had been to reduce construction and operating costs – hardly figures in today's recreations of the great days of steam.

Light railways were originally expected to be spartan and yet a lot of the obligations which the 1896 Act removed – providing signals and signal boxes, level crossing gates, station buildings, a booking office, platform staff and so on – are all part of what we expect from a 'real' steam railway. Several other aspects of the Act, had they been enforced, would have made the steam revival all but impossible. The original description of a light railway back in the 1868 Regulation of Railways Act had laid down several specific requirements, the most obvious being the restricted speed and limited axle loading.

Right and opposite: Clockwise from left: An ex-LNER Buffet Car being restored at Carnforth in the 1970s; Pooley's weighing machine at Haverthwaite station; The platform on the Lakeside & Haverthwaite Railway; Ex-BR coaches at Haverthwaite *c*. 1978; The crew of 0-6-0ST *David* pose for the camera at Haverthwaite in 1985. *David* was built in Kilmarnock by Andrew Barclay & Son in 1953 for service in Millon Ironworks on the Duddon Estuary in Cumbria. When this photograph was taken, *David* regularly hauled trains on the L&HR, but being a lightweight engine it had to work hard on the gradients – usually leading to spectacular photographs as it emerged from Haverthwaite Tunnel (see page 86).

No. 71000 *Duke of Gloucester* pulling into the platform at Carnforth in June 1991. Built at Crewe in 1954 as the prototype for a new 8P Class of locomotives but withdrawn in 1962, the Duke was eventually sold for scrap. Rescued from Barry in 1973, it was returned to steam just over thirteen years later.

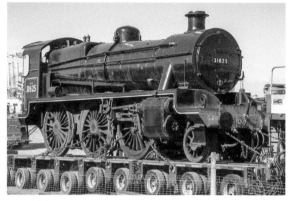

Left: Swanage Railway's U Class Mogul No. 31625 in 2016 awaiting restoration.

Below: Restored sister locomotive No. 31806 leaving Corfe Castle station in August 2018.

By reference to the earlier legislation in the appendices, those were enshrined in the 1896 legislation which, as has already been mentioned, if breached could result in fines and even imprisonment 'with or without Hard Labour, for any Term not exceeding Two Years'. For the 'escape clause' we have to refer to Clause 28 of the 1868 Act, which stated that 'A Light Railway shall be constructed and worked subject to such Conditions and Regulations as the Board of Trade may from Time to Time impose or make'. In other words, with permission, those rules could be broken.

There were a number of vaguely worded and potentially ambiguous clauses in both the 1868 and 1896 Acts, giving the Light Railway Commissioners considerable latitude in how those rules might be interpreted, as long as the primary consideration was operational safety. Arguably, they could have waived the restrictions on both the speed limit and axle loading if they believed operational safety would not be compromised.

Writing in his book *Light Railways for the United Kingdom, India, and the Colonies: A Practical Handbook Setting Forth the Principles on Which Light Railways Should Be Constructed, Worked, and Financed* (Crosby Lockwood & Son, 1896), published in the same year that the Light Railways Act was passed, John Charles Mackay offered a vision of light railways that was very close to that proposed by the Board of Trade, but a long way from the light railways which operate today.

His view was that 'a light railway is one constructed with lighter rails and structures, running at a slower speed, with poorer accommodation for passengers and less facility for freight. It can be worked with less stringent standards of signalling and safety practice. It is a cheap railway and a second class of railway'.

Today, the continuing availability of Light Railway Orders – and since 1992, their successors, Transport and Works Act Orders in England and Wales – have proved to be a highly convenient device enabling the modern heritage movement to get underway, even if the cost-saving opportunities LROs initially offered have played little part in steam preservation. As there is no equivalent of the Transport and Works Act in Scotland, Transport Scotland, on behalf of the devolved Scottish government, still issues Light Railway Orders under the 1896 Act.

Back in 1896, the maximum permissible axle loading on any railway had been determined by the type and weight of rails being used – light railways being able to use a much lighter weight and therefore cheaper rail as a means of keeping costs down. Present-day heritage lines are anything but 'a second class of railway'. They seek to encapsulate everything that helps recall the magic of the great days of main line steam. While they generally adhere to the 25 mph speed limit, there is no way that the specified 8 tons per axle loading limit could ever be achieved by a large main line locomotive and tender with a working weight of anything up to 150 tons dispersed across nine axles. But of course, today's standard gauge heritage lines use the same gauge of rails and the same substantial ballasting used on main lines, thus enabling them to support the weight of large main line locomotives and replicate that sought-after 'main line experience'.

Despite the higher construction standards of modern heritage lines, the 25 mph speed limit seems to have been accepted as inviolable – not a bad thing, really, as for most people the joy of a steam railway journey today is that gentle meander through the countryside while listening to the variety of sounds of the locomotive as its work rate changes.

Restoring rebuilt West Country Class 4-6-2 *Bodmin* – designed by Oliver Bulleid – at Quainton Road in summer 1973. The locomotive had been rescued from Woodham Brothers scrapyard in Barry in 1972, where it had lain for six years. The locomotive was built at Brighton in 1945 as No. 21C116, being given the British Railways number 34016 after nationalisation. Withdrawn from service in 1964, it was immediately sent for breaking up. Rescued in 1970 and moved to Quainton Road – now known as the Buckinghamshire Railway Centre – it was partially restored before being moved to the Mid-Hants Railway in 1976 and eventually entering service there in 1979. It was withdrawn in 1999 for a major overhaul, which was completed in 2000. It is currently undergoing another overhaul at Carnforth before perhaps returning to its home base at Swanage.

1929-built ex-GWR Class 5700 No. 5775, in London Transport colours and numbered L.89, just after being bought by the Keighley & Worth Valley Railway in 1970, is seen performing evening shunting duties at Haworth. After their GWR days were over, a number of these powerful small locomotives were subsequently sold to London Transport for overnight maintenance duties on the Underground network. Thus, No. 5775 became L.89 in 1963. In 1971 No. 5775 would become the star of the film *The Railway Children*, filmed on the K&WVR. Currently in need of a major overhaul, the locomotive is a static exhibit at Oxenhope.

There are a relatively vocal few who argue that higher speeds should be permitted under strictly controlled circumstances – and there can be no doubt that the occasional sight of a steam-hauled train running at speed on the main line certainly is something truly spectacular – but the majority of people buying tickets to travel on heritage lines do so to enjoy an unhurried couple of hours of nostalgia. The chance to see, hear and feel a train being hauled by a locomotive we may never have seen before all adds to that enjoyment – and if the trains went faster, that experience would be much shorter and infinitely less satisfying as a result.

More than half a century after the heritage movement was launched, the challenges facing the societies which operate these lines get ever more complex. The heritage movement depends heavily on volunteers, but with something as potentially dangerous as a steam locomotive, those volunteers have to be properly trained.

Above: Stanier Black 5 No. 45428 – now named *Eric Treacy* after the former Bishop of Wakefield and eminent railway photographer – standing at Pickering station on the North Yorkshire Moors Railway in the early 1990s. The locomotive was built in Newcastle by Armstrong Whitworth as one of over 300 Black 5s the company built for the LMS and entered service in 1937. Withdrawn thirty years later, it was immediately preserved. After a major overhaul, the locomotive returned to service on the NYMR in 2018, outshopped in LMS livery and carrying its original number: 5428.

Right: Caledonian Railways No. 828 at Boat of Garten station on the Strathspey Railway on a dull day in 1993, the year it returned to traffic. The 812 Class 0-6-0 is the sole survivor of an initial batch of seventeen built at the Caley's St Rollox Works in Glasgow, designed by John F. McIntosh in 1899 and numbered 812–28. It was earmarked for preservation immediately after it was withdrawn, and initially spent many years displayed at Glasgow's Museum of Transport.

Ageing locomotives are another issue, requiring ever more maintenance and that demands new generations of steam engineers with the skills to keep these beautiful machines operational. So, perhaps new builds are the key to a long-term future.

The Peppercorn A1 Class 2-6-2 *Tornado* was the first in 2008, and several other 'new builds' are in varying stages of planning and construction. Construction on a new Gresley V4 2-6-2 – No. 3403 – is in the early stages, while work on a new Henry Fowler-designed 'Patriot' Class 4-6-0, *Unknown Warrior*, has been underway now for more than a decade. It will be fitted with the first new British-built main line boiler since 1962 – *Tornado*'s boiler was built in Germany. None of the six Gresley P2 2-8-2

locomotives built in the 1930s were preserved, but a new one – No. 2007 *Prince of Wales* – is under construction at Doncaster. Work on a 'new' GWR County Class 4-6-0 is also progressing well.

Not entirely a new build, No. 1014 will be created out of two locomotives salvaged from Barry – the frames of Modified Hall Class No. 7927 *Willington Hall* and the boiler from Stanier 8F No. 48518. Slow but steady progress is also being made by the 82045 Steam Locomotive Trust in recreating a 3F 2-6-2 tank engine, more than half a century after the last of the design became one of the many hundreds of locomotives broken up at Cashmore's in Newport.

Other more unusual projects include building a late Victorian Great Central Railway Class 2 4-4-0 express engine, a new-build Great Eastern Railway Holden F5, and numerous others in varying stages of planning and construction. With just about every piece having to be made by hand, the build time of a new steam locomotive these days is measured in decades rather than years, and the patience required of their builders is quite phenomenal.

Considering what has been achieved already, however, the future for both the new generation of heritage 'light railways' in Britain and the continuation of main line steam looks reassuringly bright.

Above: A rare sight: back in the early 1990s, two of the four surviving former LMS 4-6-0 Jubilees – No. 5593 *Kohlapur* and No. 45596 *Bahamas*, built in 1936 and 1935 respectively – were in steam together on the East Lancashire Railway. At the time of writing, both are under restoration at Tyseley. The other two survivors of the class – No. 45690 *Leander* and No. 45699 *Galatea* – are both currently certificated to run on the main line, and regularly head steam specials operated by West Coast Railways.

Opposite: No. 8572 is the last survivor of Stephen D. Holden's small but powerful 4-6-0 S69 Class designed for the Great Eastern Railway, and later classified by the LNER as B12s. The GER built a total of seventy B12s in eight batches starting in 1911. After Grouping, a number of these versatile locomotives were transferred to former Great North of Scotland Railway routes, and later, after nationalisation, others could be seen hauling heavy freight trains in the south-west of England. The LNER ordered a further ten locomotives from Beyer, Peacock & Company in Manchester, and these – including No. 8572 – were delivered in 1928. The last of the class, carrying BR number 61572, was withdrawn in September 1961, having worked services around Norwich. It is fitting, therefore, that it continues to be enjoyed at work on the North Norfolk Railway today. Now owned by the Midland & Great Northern Joint Society, it is a unique engine, being the only inside-cylinder 4-6-0 locomotive in preservation in Britain. It is seen here en route from Sheringham to Holt.

Overleaf: Southern Railways Schools Class 4-4-0 No. 925 *Cheltenham* at Alresford station on the Mid-Hants Railway.

Standard Gauge Heritage Railways

These are the railways operating today under the 1896 Light Railways Act or its successors.

Aln Valley Railway

www.alnvalleyrailway.co.uk Tel: 0300 030 3311
Lionheart Railway Station, Alnwick NE66 2EZ
When the Alnmouth to Alnwick branch line – opened by the York, Newcastle & Berwick Railway in 1850 – was closed in 1968, part of the trackbed into the town was built over, and Alnwick's terminus station became a second-hand bookshop. A new terminus has been built – Alnwick Lionheart – from where they are relaying the 2.75-mile line to the coast. Currently around half a mile is operational. An application for a Transport & Works Order will enable trains to run on the remainder of the re-laid branch line.

Avon Valley Railway

www.avonvalleyrailway.org Tel: 0117 932 5538
Bitton Station, Bath Rd, Bristol, BS30 6HD
Having restored 3 miles of the Midland Railway's former Mangotsfield to Bath branch line, opened in 1869 and closed in 1966, the AVR operates trains between Oldfield Common and Avon Riverside under a 1991 LRO, using both industrial steam locomotives and heritage diesels.

Battlefield Line

www.battlefieldline.co.uk Tel: 01827 880754
Shackerstone Station, Shackerstone, Leicestershire, CV13 6NW
5 miles of the former Ashton & Nuneaton Joint Railway's line between Shackerstone and Shenton is now operational, services being provided by a mixture of steam, DMUs and railcars. Originally opened in 1873 and closed in 1965, the Shackerstone & Bosworth Light Railway Order was granted in 1981, with services recommencing shortly thereafter.

Bluebell Railway

www.bluebell-railway.co.uk Tel: 01825 720800
Sheffield Park Station, East Sussex, TN22 3QL
The railway which pioneered the whole railway heritage movement was originally built by the London, Brighton & South Coast Railway and opened in 1882. BR closed the line in 1958, long before Beeching, but by 1960 an LRO had been granted and the Bluebell became the first standard gauge heritage line in the world to carry fare-paying passengers. The 11-mile line runs from Sheffield Park to East Grinstead.

Bodmin & Wenford Railway

www.bodminrailway.co.uk Tel: 01208 73555
General Station, Bodmin, Cornwall, PL31 1AQ
Opened in 1887 and closed by BR in 1983, the former Great Western branch line from Bodmin General to Bodmin Road was reopened after being granted an LRO in 1989. The 6.5-mile line runs between Boscarne Junction and Bodmin Parkway, with trains operating on weekends from February to December and daily from May to October.

Bo'ness & Kinneil Railway

www.srps.org.uk/railway/www.bkrailway.co.uk Tel: 01506 822298
Bo'ness Station, Union Street, Bo'ness, West Lothian, EH51 9AQ
Operated by the Scottish Railway Preservation Society, the line follows part of the route of the Slamannan & Borrowstounness Railway opened in 1848 and closed by BR in 1967. An LRO was granted in 1986. Trains run between Bo'ness and Manuel. Station buildings rescued from Edinburgh Haymarket and Wormit are re-erected at Bo'ness. The Museum of Scottish Railways at Bo'ness is open daily from March to October.

Caledonian Railway

www.caledonianrailway.com Tel: 01356 622992
The Station, Park Road, Brechin, Angus, DD9 7AF
The 4-mile branch line from Brechin to Bridge of Dun was originally opened by the Aberdeen Railway Company in 1848. Passenger services were withdrawn by BR in 1952, with freight continuing until 1981. A Light Railway Order was granted in 1993, and steam trains now run on Sundays from Easter to September, diesels at other times.

Cambrian Heritage Railways

www.cambrianrailways.com Tel: 01691 728131
Old Station Building, Oswald Road, Oswestry, Shropshire, SY11 1RE
This major initiative to resurrect part of the former Cambrian Railways network in Shropshire was granted a Transport & Works Order in 2017. The original railway had been opened in 1860 and closed in 1965. The Trust has heritage sites at both Oswestry and Llynclys, and the plan is to eventually reinstate the route between the two centres.

Bo'ness station on the Bo'ness & Kinneil Railway in Central Scotland has a lot of history – the station buildings were originally at Wormit at the southern end of the Tay Bridge, while the train shed was rescued from Edinburgh Haymarket.

Chasewater Railway
www.chasewateorrailway.co.uk Tel: 01543 452623
Brownhills West Station, Pool Lane, Burntwood, Staffs, WS8 7NL
The railway – which calls itself 'The Colliery Line', recalling its industrial heritage – currently operates a 2-mile stretch of track in the Chasewater Country Park, with a roster of industrial steam and diesel locomotives. The preservation movement began in 1959, secured their site lease in 1964, and reopened services on their unique restored causeway in 1995.

Chinnor & Princes Risborough Railway
www.chinnorrailway.co.uk Tel: 01844 353535
Station Approach, Station Road, Chinnor, Oxfordshire, OX39 4ER
The former GWR branch line between Watlington and Princes Risborough opened in 1872 and was closed to passengers in 1957 and to goods in 1981. A T&WO in 1994 enabled the first section of the 3.5-mile line to reopen and the line was eventually opened as far as Princes Risborough in 2016. There are plans to extend the line to 6 miles.

Cholsey & Wallingford Railway
www.cholsey-wallingford-railway.com Tel: 01491 835067
Wallingford Station, 5 Hithercroft Road, Wallingford, Oxfordshire, OX10 9GQ
Opened in 1866, the last train to use the branch line did so in 1981, the year the Cholsey & Wallingford Railway Preservation Society was formed. An LRO was granted in 1992 and the railway now operates trains on a 2.5-mile track, largely diesel-hauled.

Churnet Valley Railway
www.churnet-valley-railway.co.uk Tel: 01538 360522
Kingsley & Froghall Station, Froghall, Staffordshire, ST10 2HA
Built in 1842 by the North Staffordshire Railway, the line was closed to passengers by BR in 1965 and to freight in 1988. The CVR was granted an LRO in 1996 and the line partly reopened that year. It was extended in stages and two-train operation became possible in 2004. Steam services operate on a 10.5-mile line from Froghall to Cheddleton.

Colne Valley Railway
www.colnevalleyrailway.co.uk Tel: 01787 461174
Castle Hedingham, CO9 3DZ
After a few years of uncertainty, and with a Heritage Lottery Fund grant behind it, the future of this project seems secure, with trains now operating on a 1-mile length of the former Colne Valley & Halstead Railway either side of the station at Castle Hedingham.

Dartmoor Railway
www.dartmoorrailway.com Tel: 01837 52762
Station Road, Okehampton, Devon, EX20 1EJ
The 15.5-mile line which is operational today forms part of the former London & South Western Railway's route from London Waterloo to Plymouth, opened in 1869. The idea behind recreating the line was to establish a community railway which would encourage

car-free visitor access to the National Park. Passenger services have been running since 1997, with trains at weekends and Bank Holidays, predominantly hauled by heritage diesels.

Dartmouth Steam Railway

www.dartmouthrailriver.co.uk Tel: 01803 553760
Queens Park Station, Torbay Rd, Paignton, Devon, TQ4 6AF
The line from Paignton to Kingswear originally opened in 1864, with passenger services being withdrawn by BR in 1972. The 7-mile route from Paignton to Kingswear was granted an LRO in 1972. The former Great Western branch line operate steam services from April to October – as well as the paddle steamer *Kingswear Castle* on the River Dart.

Dean Forest Railway

www.deanforestrailway.co.uk Tel: 01594 845840
Dean Forest Railway, Forest Road, Lydney, Gloucestershire, GL15 4ET
Originally built to broad gauge by the Severn & Wye Valley Railway in 1868 on the route of a former tramway, the line was converted to standard gauge just four years later. Closed in 1985 and reopened as a heritage railway after being granted an LRO the same year, the railway started operating passenger services on part of the route in 1986. It hopes to extend its 4.25-mile line to 6.75 miles within the next few years.

East Kent Railway

www.eastkentrailway.co.uk Tel: 01304 832042
Station Road, Shepherdswell, Dover, CT15 7PD
The original light railway was built between 1911 and 1917 by Colonel Stephens to serve the growing Kent Coalfield. All passenger services were withdrawn in 1948 and the line was finally closed in 1987. A new LRO was granted in 1993 and passenger trains ran again after more than forty years between Shepherdswell and Eythorne.

GWR 7800 Class *Lydham Manor*, a regular sight on the Dartmouth Steam Railway.

Cranmore Signal Box on the East Somerset Railway.

East Lancashire Railway

www.east-lancs-rly.co.uk Tel: 0161 764 7790
Bury Bolton Street Station, Bolton Street, Bury, Lancashire, BL9 0EY
Opened in 1846 as the East Lancashire Railway, the route was finally axed by BR in 1966. The preservation group, originally based at Helmshore, took over the line and, granted an LRO in 1986, operates over a 12-mile track between Heywood and Rawtenstall every weekend with frequent services from May to September.

East Somerset Railway

www.eastsomersetrailway.com Tel: 01749 880417
Cranmore Station, West Cranmore, Shepton Mallet, Somerset, BA4 4QP
The broad gauge line between Witham and Shepton Mallet was opened in 1858 and was closed by BR in 1965. The 2.5-mile stretch from Cranmore to Mendip Vale was reopened by the artist David Shepherd after an LRO was granted in 1974. Cranmore station's buildings were rescued from Wells and Westbury-sub-Mendip.

Ecclesbourne Valley Railway

www.e-v-r.com Tel: 01629 823076
Wirksworth Station, Station Road, Coldwell Street, Wirksworth, DE4 4FB
Opened in 1867 and closed to passengers in 1947 and freight in 1988, the 8.5-mile line between Duffield and Ravenstor – the last half-mile of which is up a 1 in 27 incline – was granted an LRO in 1996 and subsequently reopened in stages from 2002. Services are predominantly provided by a fleet of heritage DMUs and diesel locomotives.

Eden Valley Railway

www.evr-cumbria.org.uk Tel: 01768 342309
Warcop, Appleby-in-Westmorland, CA16 6P
Opened in June 1862 and, initially operated by the Stockton & Darlington Railway, the line was taken over by the S&DR just a year later. It ran, largely single-track,

from Kirkby Stephen to Clifton on the Lancaster & Carlisle Railway. Passenger services were withdrawn by BR in 1962. 2 miles of the trackbed was acquired by the EVR in 1998 and limited brake van rides from Warcop station were started in 2003. The current track length is 2.2 miles with services diesel-powered, and the railway dreams of one day reopening as far as Appleby.

Elsecar Heritage Railway
www.elsecarrailway.co.uk Tel: 01226 746746
The Railway Office, Wath Road, Elsecar, Barnsley, S74 8HJ
Currently operating on a 1-mile section of the former Elsecar Branch of the South Yorkshire Railway, plans are in hand to double the current mileage. Using industrial tank engines and Sentinel coalfield engines, the only heritage railway in South Yorkshire offers an unusual experience. Opened in 1850, the line was closed in 1984 following the closure of local collieries.

Embsay & Bolton Abbey Steam Railway
www.embsayboltonabbeyrailway.org.uk Tel: 01756 710614
Bolton Abbey Station, Bolton Abbey, Skipton, North Yorks, BD23 6AF
Operated by Yorkshire Dales Railway Museum Trust (Holdings) Limited, the 4-mile route covers part of the Midland Railway's former Skipton to Ilkley line, opened in 1868 and closed by BR in 1965. An LRO in 1981 saw the return of steam trains to Embsay station and the line was fully opened to Bolton Abbey in 1998.

Epping Ongar Railway
www.eorailway.co.uk Tel: 01277 365200
Ongar Station, Station Approach, Ongar, Essex, CM5 9BN
Opened in 1865 by the Eastern Counties Railways, at its peak this line handled fifty trains a day. It was electrified in the 1950s, by which time it was part of the London Underground network. It was axed by London Underground in 1994 and sold in 1998. Returning it to main line traffic required the trackbed to be lowered substantially under bridges. Reopened in 1994, it now operates steam and diesel on 6.5 miles of track.

Foxfield Light Railway
www.foxfieldrailway.co.uk Tel: 01782 396210
Caverswall Road Station, Blythe Bridge, Stoke-on-Trent, ST11 9BG
The 2.75-mile line from Caverswell Road station to Dilhorne Park was originally opened in 1893 by the North Staffordshire Railway to serve Foxfield Colliery. It closed in 1965 with the demise of the colliery. An LRO was granted to the preservation group in 1995, after twenty-eight years operating under the grandfather rights of the original industrial railway. Industrial steam locomotives include Haydock Foundry's 1874-built *Bellerophon*.

Gloucestershire Warwickshire Railway
www.gwsr.com Tel: 01242 621405
The Railway Station, Toddington, Gloucs, GL54 5DT

The railway operates on 14 miles of former GWR track between Broadway and Cheltenham Racecourse, using a mixture of GWR and BR locomotives. The line was opened by the GWR in 1906 and closed in 1976. An LRO was granted in 1983 before reopening in stages from 1984. The railway operates a one-, two- or three-train timetable.

Great Central Railway

www.gcrailway.co.uk Tel: 01509 632323
Great Central Station, Great Central Road, Loughborough, LE11 1RW
The Great Central operates an 8-mile section of the former London to Sheffield main line between Loughborough and Leicester, and is rare in that much of its length is double-tracked, allowing trains to pass at speed. The line was originally opened in 1897 and survived sixty-nine years until closure in 1969. Just six years later, the new GCR was born.

Great Central Railway (Nottingham)

www.gcrn.co.uk Tel: 0115 9405705
Mere Way, Ruddington, Nottinghamshire, NG11 6JS
Currently separated from the Great Central at Loughborough, the Nottingham line comprises a 10-mile section of the former GCR. There are plans to eventually reunite the two into an 18-mile heritage railway. The company currently operates under a 1992 LRO. It is anticipated that a new Order will be necessary once the two lines are reunited.

Gwili Railway

www.gwili-railway.co.uk Tel: 01267 238213
Bronwydd Arms Station, Carmarthen, SA33 6HT
The railway operates a 4.5-mile section of the former Aberystwyth to Carmarthen line from Bronwydd to Abergwili Junction, and is the only standard gauge railway operating steam services in south-west Wales. Originally opened in 1860, it was closed in 1973 and taken over by the preservation society in 1975.

Bagnall 0-6-0ST *Victor* at Washford station on the West Somerset Railway in 1987. The locomotive now operates on the Lakeside & Haverthwaite Railway following a 2015 overhaul.

Helston Railway

www.helstonrailway.co.uk Tel: 07901 977597
Trevarno Farm, Prospidnick, Helston, Cornwall, TR13 0RY
The Helston Railway originally opened in 1887 and operated on an 8-mile track, with services provided by the Great Western Railway. The line eventually closed in 1965. The Helston Railway Preservation Society was set up in 2005 and an LRO was granted in 2011. The company now operates a 1.25-mile section from Prospidnick Halt to Truthall Halt.

Isle of Wight Steam Railway

www.iwsteamrailway.co.uk Tel: 01983 882204
The Railway Station, Havenstreet, Isle of Wight, PO33 4DSY
Britain's only island-based heritage railway operates a fleet of steam and occasional diesel-hauled trains along just over 5 miles of track between Havenstreet and Smallbrook Junction. The majority of the steam locomotives and coaches are of Victorian or Edwardian origin – many having formerly worked all their lives on the island's railway network – making this a unique experience. Limited running had been started on part of the line in 1971, but the railway did not get its full LRO until 1978.

Keighley & Worth Valley Railway

www.kwvr.co.uk Tel: 01535 645214
The Railway Station, Haworth, Keighley, West Yorkshire BD22 8NJ
Operated by the Midland Railway, the line was opened in 1867 and closed by BR in 1962. Running 5 miles from Oxenhope to Keighley, it was granted an LRO in 1968 and celebrated

Left: Barclay 0-4-0ST *David* emerges from Haverthwaite Tunnel on the Lakeside & Haverthwaite Railway in the early 1980s.

Opposite above: BR Standard Class 4 4-6-0 No. 75069 in green livery at Bridgnorth on the Severn Valley Railway in the 1990s. The locomotive is currently undergoing an overhaul.

its Golden Jubilee in 2018. With over thirty locomotives, several of them steamed regularly, the K&WVR remains one of Britain's most popular railways. The railway has played a major role in several films, including *The Railway Children* and *Yanks*.

Keith & Dufftown Railway

www.keith-dufftown-railway.co.uk Tel: 01542 882123
Keith Town Station, Keith, Banffshire, AB55 5BR
Granted its LRO in 1999 and exclusively served by DMUs, the line runs for 11 miles between Dufftown and Keith Town, a thirty-eight-minute journey through spectacular scenery in the heart of Scotland's malt whisky country. Built by the original Keith & Dufftown Railway and opened in 1857, it became part of the Great North of Scotland Railway in 1866. After closure, the track was transferred from Railtrack to the Keith & Dufftown Railway Association in 1998 and services began operating in 2000.

Kent & East Sussex Railway

www.kesr.org.uk Tel: 01580 765155
Tenterden Town Station, Station Rd, Tenterden, Kent, TN30 6HE
Another line which follows part of the route of an earlier light railway – originally known as the Rother Valley Railway – whose original LRO had been granted in 1899. Colonel Stephens was directly involved and was, for a time, a director. It closed to passengers in 1961. It was granted a Light Railway (Transfer) Order in 1974, enabling it to become a heritage line, and now operates over 11.5 miles of track between Tenterden and Bodiam. The Colonel Stephens Railway Museum is opposite Tenteden station.

Lakeside & Haverthwaite Railway

www.lakesiderailway.co.uk Tel: 01539 531594
Haverthwaite Station, nr Ulverston, Cumbria, LA12 8AL
The former Furness Railway branch line to Lakeside was opened in 1869 and was axed by BR in 1965. An LRO was granted in 1973 and the railway reopened on 2 May by bishop and eminent railway photographer Eric Treacy. Steam trains run 3.5 miles between Haverthwaite and Lakeside on Windermere. L&HR operates the only preserved Fairburn 2-6-4 tanks. The railway connects with the steamer services on Lake Windermere.

Southern Railway un-rebuilt West Country Class No. 34105 under restoration at Ropley on the Mid-Hants Railway.

Lavender Line

www.lavender-line.co.uk Tel: 01825 750515
Isfield Station, Isfield, nr Uckfield, East Sussex, TN22 5XB
The Lavender Line – named not after the plant, but a local coal merchant – runs on part of the former Lewes to Uckfield Railway, opened in 1858 and closed by BR in 1969. Today trains run on a 1-mile length of track between Isfield and Little Horsted. Most steam trains are hauled by one or the other of a pair of small saddle tanks.

Lincolnshire Wolds Railway

www.llangollen-railway.co.uk Tel: 01507 363881
Ludborough Station, Station Road, Ludborough, Lincolnshire, DN36 5SQ
A Light Railway Order to authorise the partial reinstatement of the East Lincolnshire Railway between Waltham and Louth – opened in 1847 – was granted to the Great Northern & East Lincolnshire plc in 1991. So far the railway has rebuilt Ludborough station and reinstated 1.75 miles of track – a significant achievement as BR had bulldozed the buildings and lifted the track immediately after closure in 1980.

Llangollen Railway

www.llangollen-railway.co.uk Tel: 01978 860979
5 Abbey Rd, Llangollen, LL20 8SN
The 10-mile route of the Llangollen Railway – the only standard gauge heritage line in North Wales – was part of the former GWR Ruabon to Barmouth line between Llangollen and Corwen, closed by BR in 1965. An LRO was granted to the preservation group in 1980. With extensive workshops, the railway is now actively involved in locomotive rebuilds and new-builds, including a new-build of the last LMS Fowler Patriot 4-6-0, No. 5551, to be named *The Unknown Warrior*.

Mid-Hants Railway

www.watercressline.co.uk Tel: 01962 733810
Station Road, Alresford, Hampshire, SO24 9JG
Opened in 1861 and closed by BR in 1973, the Mid-Hants Railway returned to steam after the granting of the Alton & Alresford LRO in 1977. The Watercress Line runs for 10 miles from Alresford to Alton. Steam services run most weekends, and frequently in summer with a large roster of locomotives from Southern Railways, LMS and BR Southern Region. In the workshops at Ropley, the restoration of locomotives and rolling stock can be viewed up close – including the Southern Railways un-rebuilt 7P West Country Class No. 34105 *Swanage*.

Mid-Norfolk Railway

www.mnr.org.uk Tel: 01362 851723
Dereham Station, Station Road, Norfolk, NR19 1DF
11.5 miles of the southern section of the former Wymondham–Wells branch line of the Norfolk Railway was partly reopened to limited passenger services in 1997 and now operates the full length of the line under a 2001 LRO. There are plans to extend it as far as Fakenham, and perhaps eventually even to join up with the North Norfolk Railway (qv).

Mid-Suffolk Railway

www.mslr.org.uk Tel: 01449 766899
Brockford Station, Wetheringsett, Stowmarket, Suffolk, IP14 5PW
The 'Middy', as it is known, was originally approved under the 1896 Act, being granted its LRO in 1900, with amendments the following year. The line never made a profit and was eventually closed in 1952. A preservation group was set up in 1990 and a half-mile section of the line was eventually reopened at Brockford.

Middleton Railway

www.middletonrailway.org.uk Tel: 0113 271 0320
The Station, Moor Road, Hunslet, Leeds, LS10 2JQ
Now operated by The Middleton Railway Trust Ltd, this is claimed to be the oldest continuously working public railway in the world, having been established as a waggonway in 1758. Trains run on a short track of less than a mile and it has been manned by volunteers since 1960. The majority of its locomotives were built in Leeds.

Midland Railway Butterley

www.midlandrailwaycentre.co.uk Tel: 01773 747674
Butterley Station, Ripley, Derbyshire, DE5 3QZ
Operating under the Midland Railway Centre LRO of 1981, both steam and diesel-hauled trains run on the 3.5-mile track from Butterley to Hammersmith. Locomotive sheds and museum are at Swanwick, home of the Princess Royal Class Locomotive Trust. Butterley station was demolished by BR, but an identical one was moved from Whitwell in North Derbyshire and rebuilt on the site of the original.

The fireman of BR 9F 92203 – now known as 'Black Prince' – awaits the signals before running round the train at Sheringham station on the North Norfolk Railway in 2015.

Nene Valley Railway

www.nvr.org.uk Tel: 01780 784444
Wansford Station, Stibbington, Peterborough, PE8 6LR
Describing itself as 'the international railway', the NVR has an extensive collection of British, Polish, Swedish and German locomotives, and operates a 7.5-mile section of the former London & Birmingham Railway between Peterborough Nene Valley and Yarwell Junction. It was granted an LRO in 1977, and uniquely chose to become home to foreign locomotives as most of the serviceable British ones, it was said, had been acquired by other heritage railways.

Northampton & Lamport Railway

www.nlr.org.uk Tel: 01604 820327
Pitsford & Brampton Station, Pitsford Road, Chapel Brampton, NN6 8BA
The railway currently operates steam and diesel services on just under 2 miles of track between Pitsford and Brampton and Boughton. The N&LR was granted its LRO and started passenger operations in 1995. There are long-term plans to extend northwards.

North Norfolk Railway

www.nnrailway.co.uk Tel: 01263 820800
Sheringham Station, Station Approach, Sheringham, Norfolk, NR26 8RA
Built by the Midland & Great Northern Joint Railway and opened in 1887, the 5-mile route from Sheringham to Holt was reopened in 1975 under a second LRO in 1974, eleven years after closure by BR. Sheringham station retains its Victorian splendour, while Stalham station was moved from the Great Yarmouth line and rebuilt at the terminus at Holt in 2002.

North Tyneside Steam Railway

www.ntsra.org.uk Tel: 0191 2007146
Middle Engine Lane, North Shields, Tyne and Wear, NE29 8DX
The railway operates a 2-mile stretch of track from the Stephenson Railway Museum to Percy Main, using industrial steam locomotives and former BR diesels and was granted an LRO in 1991.

North Yorkshire Moors Railway

www.nymr.co.uk Tel: 01751 472508
12 Park Street, Pickering, North Yorkshire, YO18 7AJ
Opened in 1836 and closed by BR in 1965, the railway's 1971 LRO enabled it to recommence public services in 1973. The NYMR now operates a spectacular 18-mile section of the former North Eastern Railway line between Pickering and Grosmont, where there are engine sheds and a visitor centre. From late March until early November, some NYMR steam trains continue on to part of the Esk Valley line between Grosmont and Whitby, connecting Pickering with the seaside.

Peak Rail

www.peakrail.co.uk Tel: 01629 580381
Matlock Station, Matlock, Derbyshire, DE4 3NA
The railway operates on 4 miles of track between Rowsley South and Matlock Riverside, on what was once part of the Midland Railway's route from Manchester Central to London Saint Pancras. The original line was opened in 1863 and closed in 1968. Peak Rail, which runs trains between Matlock and Rowsley South, was granted its LRO in 1991, four years after the preservation group was established.

Photographed in the early 1990s at Pickering station on the North Yorkshire Moors Railway, and carrying LNER livery and numbering at the time, this K1 Thomson Peppercorn was actually built for BR in 1949. Since the late 1990s it has been in BR black, carrying its original British Railways number: 62005.

Big Pit Halt on the Pontypool & Blaenavon Railway is a short walk from the Big Pit Welsh Mining Museum.

Plym Valley Railway

www.plymrail.co.uk Tel: 07580 689380
Coypool Road, Plympton, Plymouth, PL7 4NW
When it was established in 1980, the railway's long-term goal was to restore the line from Marsh Mills to Plym Bridge, which had been closed in 1962. The railway currently operates 1.5 miles of the former Launceston branch line originally laid to broad gauge by the South Devon & Tavistock Railway in 1859.

Pontypool & Blaenavon Railway

www.pontypool-and-blaenavon.co.uk Tel: 01495 792263
The Railway Station, Furnace Sidings, Garn Yr Erw, Blaenavon NP4 9SF
Originally opened in 1866 by the Brynmawr & Blaenavon Railway, the P&BR currently operates along 2 miles of track from the site of the former London & North Western Railway's Blaenavon High Level station, past the Big Pit, to Whistle Inn. Services started on the stretch between Furnace Sidings and Whistle Inn in 1983, being extended to Blaenavon in 2010 under a 2006 Transport & Works Order. The railway's own Hunslet & Barclay industrial locomotives are occasionally augmented by visiting engines.

Ribble Steam Railway

www.ribblesteam.org.uk Tel: 01772 728800
Chain Caul Road, Preston, Lancashire, PR2 2PD
Operating along 1.5 miles of track at Preston Docks, the railway has a collection of more than forty historic industrial steam and diesel locomotives, and services operate at weekends from April to September. A Transport & Works Order was granted in 2005 and services started the following year. There are plans in hand to double the length of the line.

Royal Deeside Railway

www.deeside-railway.co.uk Tel: 01330 844416
Milton of Crathes, Banchory, Kincardineshire, AB32 5QH
Steam trains were operated for the first time in 2010 and an amended LRO was issued
in 2012. Trains now operate on 1 mile of track alongside the River Dee, part of the
former branch line from Aberdeen to Ballater constructed between 1853 and 1856 by the
Deeside Railway. Plans to extend the track length are in hand. There are a limited number
of steam days, using Barclay 0-6-0ST Salmon and two Drewery Class 03 diesel shunters.

Severn Valley Railway

www.svr.co.uk Tel: 01299 403816
The Railway Station, Bewdley, Worcestershire, DY12 1BG
The SVR's first LRO was granted in 1970, with a second coming in 1984 when the
line was extended from Bewdley to Kidderminster with its beautiful station – a replica
of the station which once stood at Ross-on-Wye. Built between 1862 and 1878, the
16 miles of which the SVR now operates was closed to passengers by BR 101 years later.

South Devon Railway

www.southdevonrailway.co.uk Tel: 0843 357 1420
The Station, Dartbridge Road, Buckfastleigh, South Devon, TQ11 0DZ
Originally built by the Buckfastleigh, Totnes & South Devon Railway, the line was opened in
1872 and closed in 1962. Now running 6.6 miles from Totnes (Riverside) to Buckfastleigh,
the SDR celebrates its 50th anniversary in 2019. Ironically, the opening ceremony in 1969
was conducted by none other than Dr Beeching himself. The original heritage operators,
the Dart Valley Railway, had been granted an LRO in 1969, and in 2002 a Transport &
Works Order was applied for by the SDR, eventually being completed in 2010.

LMS Stanier
8F No. 8233
at Bridgnorth
on the Severn
Valley Railway in
the 1990s. Built
at the North
British Works in
Glasgow in 1940,
it is currently
awaiting
overhaul.

Hunslett 0-6-0ST No. 68011 *Errol Lonsdale* (ex-WD No. 196) at Buckfastleigh on the South Devon Railway in the mid-1990s. The SDR sold the locomotive to Belgium in 2009.

Spa Valley Railway

www.spavalleyrailway.co.uk Tel: 01892 537715
West Station, Nevill Ter, Royal Tunbridge Wells, Kent, TN2 5QY
Running for 5.25 miles between Eridge and Tunbridge Wells along the former route of the East Grinstead, Groombridge & Tunbridge Wells Railway, the railway owes its existence to a merger between the Tunbridge Wells & Eridge Railway Preservation Society and the North Downs Steam Railway, which had relocated from Dartford.

Strathspey Railway

www.strathspeyrailway.co.uk Tel: 01479 810725
Aviemore Station, Dalfaber Road, Aviemore, Inverness-shire, PH22 1PY
Steam trains operate on 10 miles of former Inverness & Perth Junction Railway track from Aviemore to Boat of Garten and Broomhill under LROs granted in 1978 and 1998. The line had originally opened in 1866 and was closed to passengers by BR in 1965 and freight three years later. Trains are occasionally hauled by classic Caledonian Railways locomotive No. 828, which returned to service in 2017 after major overhaul.

BR Standard Class 4 No. 46512 prepares to leave Boat of Garten on the Strathspey Railway.

Swanage Railway's U Class Mogul 2-6-0 No. 31806 leaving Corfe Castle station for Norden.

Swanage Railway
www.swanagerailway.co.uk Tel: 01929 425800
Railway Station Approach, Swanage, Dorset, BH19 1HB
Originally opened by the Swanage Railway Company in 1885, and closed by BR in 1972, the line was partially reopened in 1980 after the granting of an LRO. Running for 6 miles from Swanage, past Corfe Castle, to Norden, and occasionally to Wareham, steam services are hauled by main line locomotives and operate daily from late March to late October, and on weekends throughout the year.

Swindon & Cricklade Railway
www.swindon-cricklade-railway.org Tel: 01793 771615
Blunsdon Station, Tadpole Lane, Blunsdon, Swindon, SN25 2DA
Running on a 2.5-mile stretch of track from Taw Valley Halt to Hayes Knoll as part of the former Midland & South Western Junction Railway, the Swindon & Cricklade Railway opened in 1884 and closed to passengers in 1964, and to freight in 1970. The railway was granted its LRO in 1984, ran its first passenger trains in 1985 and has plans to eventually extend to Cricklade and Moulton Hill.

Tanfield Railway
www.tanfieldrailway.co.uk Tel: 07508 092365
Marley Hill Engine Shed, Old Marley Hill, Gateshead, NE16 5ET
Claiming to be the world's oldest railway, with a trackbed dating in part from 1725 when a colliery waggonway was laid, the Tanfield Railway, with 3 miles of track, is home to an extensive collection of historic industrial locomotives. It currently operates under the Tanfield Railway (Causey Extension) Light Railway Order of 1991.

Telford Steam Railway
www.tanfieldrailway.co.uk Tel: 07508 092365
Marley Hill Engine Shed, Old Marley Hill, Gateshead, NE16 5ET
Telford Steam Railway operates over a mile of the Wellington & Severn Junction Railway, which was opened in 1859 and closed in 1964. The preservation group was formed in 1976 and eventually hopes to extend the line as far as the former Ironbridge Power Station site at Buildwas.

Weardale Railway

www.weardale-railway.org.uk Tel: 01388 526203
Stanhope Station, Stanhope, Bishop Auckland, Co. Durham, DL13 2YS
Operated by the Weardale Railway Trust Ltd, the company is reviving one of the oldest branch lines in the country as a heritage railway. Dating back to 1843, it was closed to passenger services in 1953 and to freight in 1991. Today trains run at weekends along the 18-mile route from Stanhope to Bishop Auckland West, a journey time of around fifty-five minutes. Currently services are diesel, but steam will be introduced as soon as NCB No. 40, built by Robert Stephenson & Hawthorn Ltd in 1954, is passed for service.

Wensleydale Railway

www.wensleydalerail.com Tel: 01677 425805
Leeming Bar Station, Leases Road, Leases Road, Leeming Bar, DL7 9AR
This stretch of the former Settle to Carlisle line opened in 1848 and was extended to Garsdale in 1878. The 22-mile preserved line from Leeming Bar to Redmire was opened in 2015, with plans to extend it a further 18 miles. Trains are mainly diesel-hauled, with steam services on selected weekends and in the summer months.

West Somerset Railway

www.west-somerset-railway.co.uk Tel: 01643 704996
The Railway Station, Minehead, Somerset, TA24 5BG
At 22.75 miles long, the WSR is the longest standard gauge heritage railway in the country, and with ten stations it offers a true GWR branch line experience. Trains runs from Bishops Lydeard to Minehead, much of it along spectacular coastline. The S&DR Trust is based at Washford station. Originally built to broad gauge and opened in 1862, the line was closed in 1973 two years after the Minehead Railway Preservation Society was set up. An LRO was granted two years later, the line partially reopening in 1976.

GWR 2-6-2T No. 4561 at Bishops Lydeard on the West Somerset Railway.